Muriel James

THE BETTER BOSS

IN

MULTICULTURAL

ORGANIZATIONS

**A Guide to Success
Using Transactional Analysis**

Marshall Publishing Company books are available at quantity discounts when used to promote products or services. For information please write to Premium Marketing Department, Marshall Publishing Company, P.O. Box 132, Walnut Creek, CA 94549.

Printed in the United States of America.

Cover and text design: Kathleen Gadway
Illustrations: John Trotta

ISBN   1 - 879369 - 00 - 1

Marshall Publishing Company
P.O. Box 132
Walnut Creek, California, 94596
Phone (415) 932-1383
Fax (415) 934-8277

Books Authored & Co-Authored by Muriel James

Born To Win: Transactional Analysis With Gestalt Experiments (Addison-Wesley Publishing, 1971)

Winning With People (Addison-Wesley Publishing, 1973)

Born To Love: *TA in the Church* (Addison-Wesley Publishing, 1973)

Transactional Analysis For Moms and Dads (Addison-Wesley Publishing, 1974)

The Power At The Bottom Of The Well (Harper & Row, 1974)

The OK Boss (Addison-Wesley Publishing, 1975)

The People Book: Transactional Analysis for Students (Addison-Wesley Publishing, 1975)

The Heart of Friendship (Harper & Row, 1976)

Techniques in TA for Psychotherapists and Counselors (Addison-Wesley Publishing, 1977)

A New Self: Self Therapy with Transactional Analysis (Addison-Wesley Publishing, 1977)

Marriage Is for Loving (Addison-Wesley Publishing, 1979)

Breaking Free: Self-Reparenting for a New Self (Addison-Wesley Publishing, 1981)

Winning Ways in Health Care (Addison-Wesley Publishing, 1981)

It's Never Too Late to Be Happy: The Psychology of Self-Reparenting (Addison-Wesley Publishing, 1985)

The Better Boss in Multicultural Organizations (Marshall Publishing Co. 1991)

Hearts on Fire: Romance In The Lives Of Great Women (Jeremy P. Tarcher, Inc. 1991)

Passion for Life: Psychology And The Human Spirit (E.P.Dutton, 1991)

This book is dedicated to Jack Howell

with deep appreciation.

Table of Contents

Acknowledgments

This book is dedicated to Jack Howell because of something
that happened in 1970. After three years of intensive work,
Dorothy Jongeward and I had completed the manuscript on
BORN TO WIN: Transactional Analysis and Gestalt Experiments.
We had tested it in a number of training seminars that we led
for business corporations and government agencies and sent it
off, with high hopes, to three publishers.

The first publisher did not answer, the second rejected it with a
formal "not interested" paragraph. The third responded with a
very paternalistic and sexist letter saying that "no one would
buy it to read, since Eric Berne had written Games People Play,
"no one would want another book on the subject even if the
book was very different." The letter went on to say, "Maybe you
girls could write something more acceptable, perhaps on family life."

Needless to say we felt devastated. At that time we knew little
about the publishing industry or what the next step might be.
One day I was pacing the floor muttering to myself, "I don't
know how to get a publisher. I guess if we're ever going to get
one, it will just have to fall down out of the blue."

At that exact moment the phone rang and a voice said, "I'm
Jack Howell of Addison-Wesley. I just fell down out of the blue
and I want to come out and discuss a contract for the manuscript you and Dorothy Jongeward wrote together."

I collapsed into a chair, took a deep breath and asked, "Who is
Jack Howell and Addison-Wesley and what do you mean by, you
'just fell out of the blue?' and how do you know about our
manuscript?"

It turned out that he had just flown in from Boston and knew
Dru Scott who was with the civil service commission at the
time. She had contracted with Dorothy and me to do a number

of training workshops for various government agencies. Dru also had a copy of our manuscript and showed it to him. Well, to make a long story short, I phoned Dorothy who lived about five miles away. She came over to my house, Jack came in from the airport and within two months we signed a contract.

During the time the book was being produced, Jack's belief in it never faltered in spite of Addison-Wesley's doubt at the time. He was told to publish it as inexpensively as possible and not print over three thousand copies.

Now, twenty years later, Born to Win continues to sell steadily — over 4 million copies have been sold in English alone. In addition, it is in sixteen languages.

Back to the story of Jack Howell. A few years after the publication of Born to Win he went to another publishing firm and we lost contact with each other. Then about a year ago a good friend of mine said she had a new neighbor who was in publishing. As they had talked about books, Born to Win was mentioned and, guess what, my friend's new neighbor was Jack Howell!

We met and talked. I told him about three phone calls I had recently received and that are mentioned in the introduction to this book. He encouraged me to respond to those calls by writing The Better Boss. So here it is, dedicated to the man who fell into my publishing life "out of the blue."

Jack is not the only one who has been part of this book. As I discussed it with friends and colleagues I found there was considerable interest and many people gave me good ideas and encouraged me in the process. I especially thank Will Svebek, Reiko Homma True, Brenda Mabry, Clint Hinton, Carol Powers, Don McKee, Dee Neuman, Ann Martin and Ellen Stegbuer.

I am also indebted to Kathleen Gadway for the design of the book. To Shoshana Alexander, Betty Fielding and Sue Hughes for their feedback and very fine copy editing, my deep appreciation.

My huband Ernest Brawley, and son John James, were also invaluable sources of references. Their personal experiences and knowledge about cultural diversity in government, business and non-profit organizations and their willingness to read and critique the manuscript was most helpful.

I also wish to acknowledge psychiatrist Eric Berne, who developed Transactional Analysis as a theory of personality and social communication. I was first introduced to him and his work 1958 and found TA to be an exciting and practical tool for helping people understand themselves and how they communicate with others.

From 1958 until his death in 1970, I met with Eric Berne and others weekly in the San Francisco Social Psychiatry Seminars. It was during these years that TA theory was clarified and expanded and I deeply enjoyed being part of the process. During these years he was also my supervisor and friend.

The International Transactional Analysis Association was founded in 1968 and continues with headquarters at 1772 Vallejo Street, San Francisco, California. It was an honor to serve as its President for two years, 1980-1981. It has also been a privilege to work with many certified transactional analysts and the regional and national transactional analysis associations. I thank them for inviting me to lecture and lead seminars in so many parts of the world. Each time I do so I am aware of my further appreciation of them.

I might not have read so extensively, worked so hard or even written this book, if it had not been for the encouragement of all of the above. Any errors or omissions are mine. None of these people are at fault and I am relieved to know that this book is only one of many to be written by other authors that will focus on the value of cultural diversity.

Introduction

The Changing Boss

The world is changing rapidly. No organization stands alone, nor does any boss. Good and better bosses are recognizing this and are also recognizing the fact that some traditional styles of management are no longer effective in this changing world. They see that some styles need to be dropped entirely, radically modified or replaced with more flexible ones. This need to change is becoming more and more apparent to those with a growing awareness of cultural diversity.

Cultural diversity has many facets, including race, gender, age, and ethnic background. Sexual preference, religious orientation and physical ability or disability are other ways cultures are sometimes defined. Understanding the similarities and differences between cultures is absolutely essential for the survival of an organization and basic humanistic values. In organizations which recognize this, bossing styles are changing.

Yet many bosses are not fully aware of the cultural differences that already exist within their organizations. They do not recognize that in successful organizations cultural barriers, like the walls between East and West Germany, are rapidly collapsing.

The collapse of some barriers between cultures has been accelerated in the United States by the world-wide movement of immigrants who seek a better life, by refugees who seek ways to survive, and by the high mobility Or many who seek better working conditions.

The Changing Culture

Recent forecasts by the U.S. Department of Labor claim that by the year 2000, eighty-five percent of new entrants into the work force in the United States will be women, immigrants, refugees and others from racial and ethnic groups which are sometimes called minorities. The word "minority" is rapidly going out of vogue because it has been used in conflicting ways. Sometimes it is used numerically and refers to a segment of the population that has fewer members than the dominant national group. Sometimes minority is used for a race or ethnic group identified by language, religion or country origin.

Sometimes women are referred to as a minority, not because they are fewer in number but because they have less power than men in the workplace. They are paid less, and have fewer opportunities for advancement.

The same Labor Department report estimates that between the years 1986 and 2000. Of those entering the workforce, 32 percent will be white, non-Hispanic males, 15 percent will be Hispanic, 13 percent will be African American and 6 percent will be Asian. Census figures are difficult to work with. To Count people by race is confusing as it is estimated that 97 percent of the Hispanics living in United States are white, yet are counted separately. However census figures often affect electoral reapportionment and many decisions about the appropriation of federal funds.

By the year 2000, 51 percent of the total workforce will be
women. and the overall employment figures will change. In
particular, the percentage of white, non-Hispanic males em-
ployed is expected to drop from 44 percent to 39 percent.
With such a diverse and changing work force, it is absolutely
necessary for managers to have more and more training in
how to work with, and value, cultural diversity. In many government agencies, business corporations, and non-profit organizations cultural diversity is becoming important. All kinds of
professional groups, from astronauts to physicists, from organizational development trainers to schoolteachers are reaching
across national boundaries. So are political action groups and
organizations established to generate friendship and understanding between people of different cultures.

In spite of this, there are many misunderstandings. Recently a
United States fast food chain opened an outlet in Eastern
Europe and expected employees to spend all their time on the
job actively working. This was contrary to their cultural style in
which they expected to have plenty of time during work to talk
with each other. Furthermore, tasks were assigned in arbitrary
ways without awareness of how culture affected performance.
The lines got longer and longer as customers waited to be noticed.

The same mistake was made in a large department store chain
in the United States when management hired sales persons
who were now immigrants who spoke English fairly well yet did
not have sufficient training and supervision on what was expected on the job. They often chatted together while customers waited in line. Although their chats were brief, they
were criticized. The problem stemmed from management's
lack of awareness and their assumptions about how entry level
employees would work although insufficient coaching had
been given.

At one time, international organizations were viewed as those
that crossed boundaries to work in "foreign" countries. That is
no longer the case. In the year 1990, one hundred and three
U.S. companies were bought by Japanese firms. In every large

city in the United States and in many smaller ones. Joint ventures are proliferating. Companies are owned by other companies that are headquartered outside the United States. These parent companies have their own executive and management styles and these styles reflect their own national culture.

Even organizations that are not controlled from outside the country have great cultural diversity. Their employees come from different regions within the nation as well as from many parts of the world. Each comes with unique customs, expectations, and assumptions. A look around any large hotel or office building shows clearly the rich cultural diversity or chaos, depending on how one chooses to see it.

Other differences are not so noticeable but they are there. People from regional subcultures also have their own expectations and ways of doing things. For instance, Californians, with their customary informality, may seem very odd to those brought up in a more formal way of life in Maine or Tennessee, Pennsylvania or Texas. The challenge in recognizing and dealing with such differences is an important task for anyone in a management position.

The Origin of Cultural Diversity in USA

Even the briefest reading of U.S. history shows that every wave of immigrants or refugees brings its own cultural values and the emerging trend is to recognize that United States is a pluralistic society and always has been. Native Americans were tribes with their unique subcultures and in the census were recognized as such because they were different.

According to historian David H. Fisher, the early settlers from England also had very different cultures and different values, and were not at all homogeneous. When some immigrated to Virginia, for example, they brought their servants and continued to live a life style to which they were accustomed. Others came in poverty, settled in different parts of the new country and developed culturally diverse life styles. All they had in common was the English language and the desire to be self-determining.

The French also hoped for American colonies. They did not succeed in taking over the English ones, but they did settle in the Southern Mississippi valley and acquired vast lands from the Spanish in the middle of the continent. In 1803 Napoleon sold this land to the United States as the Louisiana purchase to to finance his wars. Meanwhile the influence of the French culture remained strong around New Orleans.

During the 1800's, immigration remained high as people came for adventure or to get rich, or because of political or religious persecution or hunger. In 1846 over a million died of hunger in the Irish potato famine and many of the survivors immigrated. Later great numbers of Jews came from Poland and Russia to escape being massacred.

There were many other important population movements that have led to cultural diversity in United States. From 1840 to 1850, about a million German farmers and artisans immigrated to escape extreme hardship in Germany. In fact, so many Germans had already settled in Pennsylvania that Benjamin Franklin had been concerned that they might be a divisive element in the development of the country because they continued to speak German instead of English.

Incidentally the same concern continues today about others who do not speak English, and considerable debate and legislation is involved in trying to work out the problems of political equality for citizens who do not speak a common language. Economic and social difficulties are inherent in this and must be addressed. This is being done in some places. In San Jose, California, all city employees who are bilingual in Spanish or Vietnamese, for example, receive higher pay than those who are not. The same is true in San Francisco with those who speak Chinese, Japanese, Tagalou, Spanish, Cambodian, and Vietnamese.

The word "Hispanic" is used to denote Americans of Spanish or Latin American origin or descent. Their common bond is the Spanish language. Their cultural backgrounds are often radically different.

Originally Spaniards came to the New World in the 16th Century, long before other groups, to explore, conquer, settle and Christianize the native populations. Spain soon controlled much of North and South America. In 1819, Spain and the United States finally agreed on which country would control what. For example, United States agreed on Spanish rule over Texas, and Spain gave up its control over Oregon and Florida.

Then Mexico revolted from Spain and won its independence in 1824. Next, Texas revolted and won its independence from Mexico to become a republic with a large Spanish, Mexican and slave population. Later it voted to become a state. Meanwhile, as a result of wars and revolutions, New Mexico and California were ceded to the United States.

Beginning in about 1930 there was another large influx of Mexicans who came, legally or illegally, to work on the railroads and in agriculture. Since then, people of many parts of Latin America have immigrated to the United States sometimes as refugees seeking safety from oppressive governments, sometimes as immigrants hoping for a better standard of living.

In 1898 Puerto Ricans began moving to the U.S. in large numbers, about 80 percent of them to New York. The Cuban immigration, much more recent, started in 1959 when Fidel Castro's rise to power led to an economic as well as a political exodus as many wealthy Cubans fled.

The immigration of Asians into the United States began in the 1860's with mostly men to be laborers and farmers and only a few women. Until as late as 1922 people who were descendents of any culture could own land except the Japanese and Chinese. In 1924 further Asian immigration was banned. Asians had been useful when they worked for low wages in agriculture and on the railroads but were seen as a threat when they became successfully self-employed.

Although Asians in the US are racially the same, their histories and cultures are different. They came from different countries and even today many prefer to be identified not racially, but as Chinese, Korean, Filipino, Japanese or Japanese American or some other designation that refers to their own country of origin.

The most glaring example of discrimination against immigrants occurred during World War II when Japanese American citizens, especially those in the western states, were interned in camps. They were not so treated in Hawaii where a large percentage of the population was of Japanese descent.

In the far Northwest different cultures also existed. The original occupants of Alaska were Eskimos and American Indians who were first ruled by the Russians. Bought from the Russians in 1867, Alaska was made a territory and then a state. As a last wilderness with all the economic opportunities and natural beauties that are there, it draws immigrants from many cultures.

A Personal Note

Although economic, social and political power has been mainly in the hands of white male leaders, the US has always been culturally diverse. My own interest in this began in early childhood and indirectly is associated with Alaska, through my maternal grandmother. Long before I was born she had gone with my grandfather to Alaska during the gold rush of the late 1800's. With the gold they brought back they built a very large and lovely home in Berkeley, California, only one block from the university. However, building the house took everything they had. Grandfather died young and grandmother, who loved the house but could not afford it, had it remodeled into small apartments for university students.

When I visited my grandmother as a child, I often hid behind a sofa as she was interviewing prospective renters with different accents, skin and hair color, clothes and shapes of eyes. She first asked about their academic studies and then what else interested them. When I queried her why she did so, grandma answered, "If people are interested in several things they will not be bored and neither will I. I like to talk to people who know things that I don't know as I can learn from them." Evidently, her interest in cultural diversity was passed on to me.

My parents moved from Berkeley to San Francisco when I was three years old. There I went to public schools which were ethically mixed and my grandmother's attitude was reinforced by my parents. My mother was a concert pianist; my father a scientist as well as an organist. Although they were busy with their own lives and I was frequently ignored as a child, I often sat on the stairs going up to the second floor where I could watch and listen to many different kinds of people, sometimes using different languages, coming and going with their musical instruments or discussing scientific papers.

As I reflect on those days I realize that I had little awareness of racial and ethnic barriers. Among people who had common interests the cultural differences were interesting, not irritants.

It was not until 1957 that I began to analyze some differences. At that time the Russians entered space with the launching of Sputnik. Suddenly United States educators interpreted this as a threat to national security so curriculums were quickly changed to include more mathematics and science. At the time I was doing graduate studies at the University of California and was intrigued with the concept of how one event in one culture can so rapidly create changes in other cultures. In fact I became so fascinated that I wrote my doctoral dissertation on the effects of national and international crises in ancient history. The subject still fascinates me but, as one of my friends recently remarked, "Don't get Muriel started on that or she'll never stop!"

Another significant time in my life that reinforced this lifetime interest was when, in 1957, I was invited to Bossey, Switzerland to share seminar leadership in a group of about thirty persons who were leaders in literacy education in third world countries. As we lived and talked and planned together something happened to me, a global dimension was added to my life. At a very deep level I seemed to become a citizen of the world.

Other events occurred that influenced me. In the 1960's issues of civil rights were emerging strongly. Although as a child I experienced many other ethnic cultures, I did not know what it was like to be black. My concern for voting rights for everyone led me to Selma, Alabama in 1964, to march with Martin Luther King, Jr. and begin to understand the tragedy of rampant discrimination.

After this I was part of a task force that was funded by the Ford Foundation with the University of California and under the leadership of Dr. Marie Fielder. We were a group of eight persons of different racial backgrounds whose task was to go into high schools and de-escalate potential interracial violence that was growing especially after the assassination of Martin Luther King Jr. During this time my awareness was heightened further by the stories I heard and the experiences I had while lecturing and leading workshops for many kinds of organizations in many countries.

Another part of my growing cultural awareness was as a consultant to the California Commission on the Status of Women. Like many women I had personally experienced discrimination on many jobs. It was usually expressed in the form of lower pay and less opportunities for advancement. Being part of this commission and their public hearings brought me face to face with other forms of cultural prejudice. For example, a woman over forty had great difficulty being accepted into doctorate programs at universities. Although many of these issues have been resolved by law, by custom they still exist.

The Purpose of This Book

I had never intended to write this book but in the spring of 1990 three phone calls within one month led me to make the decision to do so. One call came from a major corporation that handles government contracts. The other two calls came from large international businesses. Each of them wanted to order hundreds of copies of one of my books, *"The OK Boss"*, that was published in 1975. However, it was out of print.

Because they asked for so many copies I toyed with the idea of having it reprinted. Then I looked at it and decided it was out of date and thought of revising it. As I studied it further, all my interest in the value of multiculturalism seemed to flood me. I started an intensive study on some of the issues current today. I talked to innumerable people, observed what was going on in many different kinds of organizations, and reviewed much of the current writing on the subject. Gradually this book took shape with some of the format from my previous book but with a very different focus.

Cultural diversity in the United States is a complex subject. The examples used in this book are not inclusive, nor is the suggested reading list. They are intended to illustrate three particular points: (1) that we are all immigrants or refugees, or descendants of people who came out of choice or we are descendants of indentured servants or slaves who had no choice when they came; (2) that if we do not already value cultural diversity in ourselves and others, we can learn to do so and (3) we can work so that these positive attitudes add to our effectiveness and efficiency.

Immigration is bound to continue and it will also continue to change our already pluralistic culture. We must hurry to keep pace. An Wang, an immigrant whose success story in computers and in establishing Wang Laboratories is well known. His policy is that if a male employee had trouble with women, then his company does not need that employee. Furthermore adds Wang's Director of Human Relations, "If you're a salesperson and you have hang-ups about dealing with people of color, if you have problems selling to a black, you're going to lose money for the company, and we don't need you."

The purpose of this book is to help managers recognize the diverse cultures that are prevelant but often ignored, to value such diversity, and to increase skills for functioning creatively and effectively with people who are similar in some ways and different in many.

To function effectively, every manager needs to understand and be able to use seven essential managerial skills. They are directing, coaching, delegating, analyzing, peacemaking, defending, and innovating.

To assist the process of learning how to use these skills, Transactional Analysis, often abbreviated TA, will be included as a tool for understanding the dynamics of cultural diversity and how to communicate more effectively.

Although TA was originally developed for psychotherapists to help people understand themselves and their communication patterns, the application of Transactional Analysis has been greatly expanded. Innumerable business corporations, government Agencies and non-profit organizations have discovered the value of TA. Books on the subject have been translated into eighteen languages and it is currently used as a training tool in eighty-five different countries.

This kind of popularity is clear evidence of the value of TA for those who wish further understanding on how to be better bosses in multicultural organizations. At the end of each chapter some practical exercises are included so that cultural diversity can be seen not as an inconvenience, but as a valuable resource in every organization.

I hope the book makes a difference in your life and work.

Muriel James
Lafayette, California

1

Management skills for today

Everyone a boss

Everyone has some control over their work and their personal lives. Therefore, everyone is a boss. The word "boss" is a colloquial term for master. It is often used for those who have others under their direction or control.

Boss does not mean the same as a phrase which denotes skill, such as "master craftsman." The word "boss" stresses authority rather than capacity. It is used for supervisors, managers, and top executives. The question, "Who's the boss around here?" is sometimes used by strangers who want to make contact with the person in charge, or it is used to argue about the role of an authority. When people are labeled "bossy" it means they have overstepped the limits of good management practices and are exploiting a position of authority, or trying to do so.

This can occur at any level in an organization. Traditionally, the supervisor's job is considered the management of people and the solving of problems related to the particular jobs. The manager's job is generally more diversified. It is to set objectives, to organize personnel and resources in order to achieve these objectives, and to establish ways of measuring the degree of success or failure. The executive's job is to stay aware of the larger plan of the organization, make global decisions, manage the managers, and deal with some of the overriding tough issues that face organizations in today's world. At every level of management, it is the job of every boss to motivate employees and help them develop their skills.

In actual practice, the supervisors, managers, top executives, corporation officers and board of directors all deal with people — both as bosses and as subordinates. Almost everyone in an organization has some kind of bossing responsibility for someone else. Each also has a subordinate relationship to someone else. Even corporation officers have to please others — the board of directors, the stockholders, and, ultimately, the consumers — if an organization is to survive.

Being a good boss is not always easy. And being a better boss is even more challenging. Unfortunately, many organizations have poor or mediocre bosses.

Poor and mediocre bosses

The poorest bosses in any organization are those who restrict the skills, capacities and personal development of their employees and do not recognize the many different cultures they must deal with in a rapidly changing workplace.

They are often rigid in their beliefs and opposed to organizational change unless they personally initiate it. They tend to think of themselves as highly competent when, in reality, they may be smugly superior and have an inflated view of their own importance.

Mediocre bosses are somewhat better than poor ones as they may try to help their employees. However, they are not very potent. Nor are they particularly interested in updating their information or skills. Not knowing or caring about cultural diversity and change, they act as if the world is still the way it was many years ago.

Good and better bosses

Good bosses are continually in the process of evaluating themselves so that they can become more effective. They are committed to what they consider to be worthwhile work. They are doers as well as dreamers, pioneers as well as planners. Their work is part of their identity and contributes to their own well-being and that of others.

Better bosses are those who become leaders. Whether they supervise a small group of employees or manage a division within a large organization, they envision goals, affirm values and motivate others to accept similar positive goals and encourage their subordinates to succeed.

They are also experts at dealing with change. They recognize and appreciate cultural diversity and continually update their own skills and those of their employees to be more effective in coping and instigating change. Updating requires attention to details.

Good and better bosses know and value cultural diversity and update their own skills, as well as the skills of subordinates, so that they can be more effective in dealing with change. They know recognizing global change is essential to good management.

These kinds of bosses see that even among employees of the same race, gender, and ethnicity there is a wide diversity. Words, gestures, facial expressions, and work styles reveal time and again that every individual is unique. They are different because of what is inherited genetically, what is passed down culturally from generation to generation, and the social conditioning that is experienced throughout life.

Better bosses, who are always in the process of updating themselves, recognize that even people who live in the same large city often have different subcultural values. From one part of the city people may speak and dress in one way, while those from another part may look and act according to a different subculture. Everybody brings their own subculture to work.

Better bosses are also aware that every organization has its own unique culture which includes traditions of how to behave toward superiors, subordinates and peers, whether to take initiative or just wait for orders, whether to work intensely or casually, and many other expectations, including how to dress. When employees do not understand and value cultural diversity, discrimination may flourish. The better bosses discourage discrimination in any form.

Better bosses often take time and energy to explore their own cultural values as well as those of others. They become increasingly aware of how these values affect behavior. They honor diversity. They become leaders who do not wait passively for things to happen. Instead, they motivate others, initiate change, and constantly are concerned with establishing fair practices and building morale. They use their time creatively and productively and separate the important from the unimportant.

Bossing skills and styles

Different jobs call for different skills. Those which are most necessary to bosses are directing, coaching, delegating, analyzing, peacemaking, defending and innovating.

These seven bossing skills are task-oriented and can be used either in negative ways by poor or mediocre bosses, or in positive ways by those who are good or better bosses. The ways they are used is what improved management is all about. The skills and the opposite ways they are used are as follows:

Directing:
> From demanding to discerning

Coaching:
> From interfering to encouraging

Delegating:
> From neglecting to empowering

Analyzing:
> From unfeeling to caring

Peacemaking:
> From appeasing to negotiating

Defending:
> From bullying to advocating

Innovating:
> From confusing to creating

Whereas some supervisory, management and executive positions call for using only one of these skills on a regular basis, most jobs require a combination of skills. If these are not developed, then bossing is not as effective as it could be.

It is common for people to assume on scanty evidence that there is a "best" way to be a boss — usually their way. If they discover that their way is not the best for all people in all situations, they may excuse themselves by saying, "That's just the way I am" or justify their position with, "This is what bossing is all about." When such bosses discover that their limited skills are not sufficient, they can decide to learn new ways to become better bosses.

Better bosses are those who easily shift from one managerial skill to another according to the situation, or those who deliberately combine skills when appropriate. New employees often need a boss who acts like a coach when they start a new job. After learning what is expected, they may respond better to bosses who are skillful at delegating authority and who empower them without constantly checking up on them and giving them more help than they need or want.

However, the usefulness of any management skill depends upon the situation in which it is used. What is sometimes a healthy detachment when delegating something to employees can turn into a major disaster when something unusual happens such as when oil tankers split open or nuclear reactors explode.

Bosses can improve their own skills and the skills of those they manage. What they have not yet learned can be learned. Poor or mediocre bosses can improve at managing others and good bosses can get even better.

Directing:
from demanding to discerning

Most supervisory, management, and executive jobs call for directing others. This is the oldest and most traditional bossing skill, and it can be used poorly or brilliantly.

Demanding Directors are poor bosses who, like political dictators, believe only in their own opinions and are constantly critical and demanding of others. They are nagging, repressive, and opinionated parental-types who insist on things going their way. Seldom open to new ideas or new procedures, they are highly dogmatic. "That's the way it's always been and that's the way it's going to be," insists this type of boss.

If changes are made in the organization, the changes are often extensions of the Demanding Dictator's previously held traditions and prejudices. Resentful of those who might want some power and authority of their own, this kind of boss can undermine an organization's potential progress with the strongly held belief, "I'm the boss and I know what's best." Others may not agree.

Because of the rigidity in their thinking, these kinds of bosses often have more difficulty than others in dealing with employees who have different cultural values than they do. They prefer people of like background who jump to attention when they say, "Do it now."

When a critical, authoritarian type is prominent in non-profit organizations such as schools and hospitals, morale declines, mistakes become more common, and there is a general unrest. In volunteer organizations such as the Red Cross, scouts, or museum guilds, this kind of boss is a disaster. Non-paid workers will often quit their volunteer activities and go where they are more appreciated. In the family, the most basic organization in the world, this style usually elicits frightened compliance or strong rebellion.

In contrast, the better boss is a *Discerning Director.* These bosses manage others from positive points of view. They are observant, informed and astute. Although they criticize, they are fair critics who can give reasonable directions without shouting or ridiculing. They are able to judge, discuss, discern, and communicate their expectations. Like a good theatrical critic who competently evaluates a stage play, these bosses can see what is good and what is poor in the workplace and criticize in tolerable ways. Few subordinates want to be criticized by a supervisor, manager or the CEO, yet many jobs call for correcting behavior so the challenge is how to do it well.

Some discerning directors are on the cutting edge in organizations because they constantly update their information. They listen well and open-mindedly consider pros and cons so they seldom make erratic or irrational judgments. Though they can be critical, their criticism is usually based on factual information, not on opinions formed from incomplete data or cultural bias. They have the ability to discern between the important and the unimportant and direct others with clear instructions.

Bosses such as these are valuable in every kind of organization and tend to maintain only traditions which they have thought through and consider to be useful. They set limits so that employees know what is expected, and this provides a sense of direction and security. They are the ones who often insist on getting things done and getting them done on time. They work well under pressure. Such bosses often expect a lot from people and, consequently, often get a lot.

Coaching:
from interfering to encouraging

Coaching is a form of advising and may be done well or poorly by bosses, trainers, teachers or others who have the responsibility for developing subordinates. Many jobs call for a boss who is able to coach well.

When bosses are good at this they are usually supportive, parental types who take pleasure in helping others learn how to do their best and how to get ahead. Whether they are supervisors or managers, teaching individuals or groups, some of the best trainers in business, government, and non-profit organizations have mastered the fine skill of coaching.

Interfering Coaches have not learned how to do this. Instead of training employees to develop personally, as masters train their apprentices, they can slow down their employees' progress by interfering in their work when requiring unnecessary reports. Instead of training a group to work together as a team, as an athletic coach would do, they sometimes set one employee against another. Or they may interfere in employees' private lives without being asked to do so.

Such bosses often think of themselves as benevolent, but they can overwhelm others by trying to prevent any possible mistake. They are so busy being helpful that they smother independence. They mind other people's business instead of their own and constantly check up on others like over anxious parents.

Although they appear to be like nurturing parents, underneath the mask there is often a paternalistic attitude.

Pretending to care, they actually enjoy feeling superior and tend to keep others "in their place" instead of encouraging them to become competent.

Unfortunately, bosses of any race or ethnic background are often condescending to those of a different race or ethnic background. They may do the same with physically handicapped or inexperienced employees. If the bosses are men managing women, they may assume that women are helpless and incapable of clear, independent thought and action.

Encouraging Coaches use more positive coaching skills. They encourage teamwork and demonstrate new strategies that can be used on the job. They cheer others on with brief pep-talks and do everything possible to help them develop their potential. Pleased with the successes of their department or division, they do not try to elevate themselves by taking all the credit.

They are sincerely concerned over subordinates and offer them opportunities for training that could lead to advancement. Even beyond that, they are often concerned over issues of health and safety and encourage employees to work as a team to facilitate positive changes in these areas.

Bosses who are good coaches are usually patient when giving instructions. They are willing to repeat them if they're not understood, and are flexible enough to change strategies if that seems appropriate. They listen well and give active feedback. They support others with appropriate advice and sympathy. As a consequence, employees tend to feel understood and often respond with higher motivation and productivity.

Delegating:
from neglecting to empowering

Delegating authority and responsibility is an important management task. It can be neglected so that the power doesn't go with the assignment but remains with the assignor, or is given away haphazardly to get rid of the task, or handled carefully to get the work done well.

Neglecting Delegators are bosses who pretend to work but are essentially uninvolved. When delegating tasks, they make their assignments carelessly or not at all. They neglect thinking about who might have the time or skills to do the tasks efficiently.

Because of their basic indifference, these bosses do not relate well to others. Neither critical nor nurturing, they prefer distance. In planning sessions they may act as if an issue being discussed is important to them when actually they "couldn't care less."

Whether such a boss is a supervisor of a typing pool, personnel director of a corporation, or chief petty officer in the navy, this kind of boss is essentially indifferent toward the organization and toward others. They are like bystanders, unconcerned over quality control. Bosses who are neglectful at the job of delegating are also neglectful about becoming aware of important changes due to cultural diversity.

In educational organizations where they may have tenure, or in government agencies and business where retirement pay is certain, these supervisors and managers are innumerable. They are the ones leaning on their shovels while the rest of the crew does the work. They may act "cool as cucumbers" yet only be marking time until Friday or retirement. This kind of boss may just shuffle papers around and occupy the job instead of doing it.

Often loner types, if they have private offices, they keep their doors closed, use large desks, and tip-back chairs. The chairs for visitors are often set at a distance or are uncomfortable enough to convey a "don't stay" message. Sometimes their desks are clear but more often are piled high with papers as a nonverbal announcement of how hard they are working — no matter how much they are neglecting the job.

In contrast, *Empowering Delegator* bosses are liberating. They allow others the freedom to work at their own pace, set their own limits, design their own goals, develop their own programs, and run their own show. An increasing number of large corporations have discovered the value of delegating, even at the top levels, and have allowed whole divisions to become autonomous, thus improving motivation and morale.

One of the noticeable characteristics of Empowering Delegators is that they tend to trust other employees to get the job done. They make reasonable assignments, stay out of other people's way, and maintain a somewhat "hands-off" policy. They clearly expect good work and allow it to be done without hovering over their employees.

They are usually flexible in scheduling deadlines and are neither overly helpful nor critical. They empower others with authority and responsibility and expect them to be creative, loyal and competent. Self-motivated employees thrive in the liberating climate that this kind of delegating boss provides.

Analyzing:
from unfeeling to caring

The task of analyzing budgets, products, services and personnel is necessary for organizations to establish goals and achieve them. Without the proper use of such skills, financial failure is an ever-present possibility.

Unfeeling Analyzers are bosses who can analyze hard data very well but are not sufficiently programmed for the human side of management. They analyze for the sake of analyzing and are so intent on processing data that they are like unfeeling machines. To them, people are like merchandise stacked in a warehouse meant only to be bought and sold or discarded if not perfect for the task as defined in the program. These bosses do not live by ethical principles and may be negligent in

complying with anti-discrimination laws because they are programmed to seek only financial profit.

In the extreme form, when recruiting new employees, this boss
may send out memos about endless job security and benefits to
be paid for by the organization yet lay off loyal employees
shortly before their retirement to avoid paying retirement
benefits.

Cultural diversity has no value to them unless it brings in
money. They may hire the fewest possible workers of a particular racial or ethnic background, or they may hire many of them
if they see that such employees can be exploited.

Bosses who calculate everything seldom show sympathy and
concern for others. They act as if they had lost the ability to
laugh and enjoy or to be nurturing or caring. If an employee
brings up a personal problem, they may say things like, "The
job is no place to discuss personal problems," or even worse,
"It's not my problem that your kids are sick. We're busy and
can't save your job if you take time off. Perhaps you'd better
look for another one." This kind of mechanized, ruthless response does nothing to promote efficient work or organizational loyalty.

In contrast, a *Caring Analyst* is the better boss who is effective
because of analytical abilities to collect data, process it, and es-
timate probabilities with humanistic values in mind. For example, when an employee requests time off because of a sick
family member, this boss does not respond with hostility or indifference but tries to imagine what it would be like to be in
that situation and then tries to work out an acceptable solution. Bosses who are caring analysts realize how important a
family member's health can be in keeping an employee fully
functional.

These bosses recognize the importance of employees and the
value of retaining experienced employees, including those
with young children. They do things such as recommending
that day care centers be established by their organization, and

adjacent to it, because they believe this convenience allows parents to concentrate on working and thus builds loyalty to a company that respects and serves them.

Bosses who are caring analysts do not function like computers. They have a humanistic programming which is sophisticated enough to include the complexity of reality. In communicating with others, they deliberately try to speak and write clearly. In workplaces where for some employees English is used as a second language, they deliberately speak more slowly, avoid jargon and colloquialisms, and ask employees to give them feedback to see if they are being understood.

They will make similar attempts to understand the employees and also ask for clarification if they don't understand. Although some employees may be reluctant to give feedback, when they know the boss sincerely wants to understand, they will feel more comfortable using a feedback process.

Caring and analytical bosses also use time productively because they know its value and agree that there is a time for work and a time for play and that distinguishing between the two is important.

Peacemaking:
from appeasing to negotiating

Although not all jobs call for peacemaking on a regular basis, most bosses need to use this skill at times, whether they are negotiating vacation schedules, or raises in salary, or settling issues of discrimination. When peace is negotiated between countries or companies, between departments or individuals, it is because those involved have been able to focus on the issues and reach some kind of compromise.

Appeasing Peacemakers often actually undermine peacemaking negotiations that have the potential for being successful. They feel insecure and do not have strong bargaining powers. Consequently they are ineffective in mobilizing human resources or getting employees the benefits to which they are entitled.

They tend to give in to their own bosses or aggressive subordinates, and often act servile while trying to please everyone, though they seldom succeed.

These bosses are often so fearful of conflict that they go to great lengths to avoid any kind of confrontation, saying such things as, "Let's not get upset. It will all work out in time and arguing won't get us anywhere." This kind of conciliatory stance irritates those who prefer a more direct approach to interpersonal problemsolving and who might even appreciate loud and demanding voices in some situations.

In contrast, *Negotiating Peacemakers* are often successful bosses who know their values, are ethical and respect cultural differences. Whether in minor supervisory roles or in major management positions, this kind of boss is willing to look at both sides of arguments and skillfully work for reasonable solutions.

Many issues, such as minimum wages and the use of child labor that once led to bloody battles between management and labor unions, have been settled by law. Now the issues that often need to be negotiated are salary increases, sick leave, and health and retirement benefits. Human resources directors, supervisors and managers, are also called upon to negotiate short-sighted practices such as unsafe working conditions. They are also called upon to make peace when conflict occurs between employees.

Negotiating peacemakers often use group processes and involve employees at many levels when making decisions. This is especially useful when there is a possibility of explosive tempers or impulsive action. Group process can greatly assist decision making. One of its goals is to use diverse points of view to come to a satisfactory synthesis in problem solving.

Obviously, using group process for decision making is more time consuming than when decisions are made by one person.

Yet peacemakers who are negotiating seldom use threats to speed up the process. They know that intimidation is likely to elicit defensiveness instead of cooperation, and they believe that cooperation is crucial to the effective resolution of conflict. Increased attention is being given to this way of bossing because of the effect of the Japanese style of management.

Japanese firms are known for their emphasis on group consensus, so in companies owned by Japanese organizations many managers and supervisors are learning to use group leadership skills.

Even if negotiators do not use group process, they are often effective in interpersonal conflicts between employees because they listen to other people's feelings and opinions. Those involved feel they can relax and be more honest with such bosses. They sense they will be respected as persons, even if they disagree on some issues. In the atmosphere created by this kind of boss, misunderstandings can be clarified, conflicts can be negotiated, and problems can be solved.

Defending:
from bullying to advocating

Defending one's subordinates against unfair practices is a management skill that is used in many situations where advocacy is important. To advocate is to intercede and speak up in favor of someone else. In the process of providing this kind of support to employees, the good and better bosses sometimes defend the values of their subordinates even when these values are not the same as those held at the executive level.

Bullying Defender bosses are those who are hostile to administration or to subordinates or to both. They attack others and defend only themselves or those who agree with them. They like to fight.

These bosses often have a lot of unresolved anger which may be openly expressed with shouting and threats or thinly disguised with sulkiness, deceitfulness and procrastination. This is often true with bosses who postpone setting vacation schedules, establishing budgets, discussing personnel problems, and so forth.

Anger disguised is also expressed by employees who are not committed to time schedules and wish they were somewhere else doing something else. If such people are confronted on their procrastination they often come back with sarcasm and harbor resentment about it for a long time.

When hostility becomes more open, belligerent bullies often go for revenge. They may try to get particular individuals fired or discriminate in some way against all who belong to the offending sex or race or ethnic background. Their ignorance and prejudice are threats to the health of any organization.

The *Advocating Defender* type of boss can be very assertive but is not basically hostile. When defending ideas, procedures or employees, such bosses are willing to insist on what they want and do not give in to others easily. They are able to make clear why their department budgets and personnel are necessary and should not be cut.

These bosses respect their subordinates and show them new strategies and techniques while advocating growth and change. They share pertinent information with employees and trust them to be discreet and make good use of it. They act with integrity and refuse to take unfair advantage over others, even those who are opposed to their ideas.

In any kind of situation calling for defense of their interests they take time to understand their own national and company culture and recognize that what might be useful in one situation may not be effective elsewhere. Although they learn the value systems and customs of others, they assertively speak out in favor of their own organizations.

Innovating:
from confusing to creating

The management skill of innovation is the skill of making changes successfully. It often involves modernizing a organization or recasting its goals or restyling the way it functions. The central focus is on change.

To innovate also means to invent or to introduce a new product, process or idea. Creative innovation is the basic process developing a new product or marketing plan. It is basic to changing the model of a car that is being manufactured, a curriculum that is being taught, or a government that is being reformed. There is no end to the necessity for creative innovations.

However, bosses who are *Confusing Innovators* do not recognize that innovations usually require time, energy, and funds. These bosses are so hungry for praise that they often act scatter-brained and like reckless reorganizers. They lack the interpersonal skills that are necessary for carrying out innovations. "Let's try something new" or "Lets get reorganized" is their constant refrain, whether what they suggest is practical or not.

Bosses who are confused themselves naturally confuse others. They do not think through the process of change and what the costs might be in terms of products, personnel and services. They may have fantastic goals, often copied from someone else, but lack ways to implement them. They tend to want change just for sake of change. They hope that any change will be an improvement and say to themselves, "After all, that new software company is doing it a new way, so maybe we should copy it, if we could just find out how to do it."

They may reorganize a department, division, agency or company with reckless energy and try to convey the idea that they are creative when actually they may not have had an original idea in decades. Their often frantic excitement is seldom clarifying.

Creative Innovators, on the other hand, use their positive bossing skills to initiate change. These bosses are well liked for their ready flow of fresh ideas and enthusiasm that energizes others. "I've got a great idea," one might say, "and I think I know how we could do it."

They can be counted on to dream up real solutions for old problems, new designs for outmoded equipment, and new policies, programs, and procedures that others can readily implement. They find ways to draw upon cultural diversity because they know that creative and innovative skills are universal.

Knowing that creativity exists in everyone, they also solicit ideas from the work force as a whole and encourage the upward flow of new ideas to bosses who make the major decisions.

When some employees are uncomfortable with creative changes in products, services or marketing, the innovative boss tries to find establish a climate in which they will feel more comfortable. With employees who are already comfortable with change, the innovative boss is stimulating.

Effective and efficient bosses

Whereas some bosses are comfortable using one kind of bossing behavior, others flip back and forth into several of the common patterns. For example, a given boss may act like a dogmatic dictator with some employees, like a discerning director with others, like a encouraging coach at some times, and like a negotiator who wants peace at other times. And necessarily so. The ability to change is an important factor in effectiveness and efficiency.

Peter Drucker, in his classic book, *Management*, claimed that "Effectiveness is the foundation of success. Efficiency is a minimum condition for survival after success has been achieved." Organizations that work well have to do both the right thing (the goal) and do the thing right (the procedure).

For a person with an inflamed gall-bladder, surgery can be the right thing. Doing the surgery with skill is doing it right.

Developing a new product may be the thing to do and it may also call for some employees to work long hours without enough sleep. But driving them hard week after week is not doing it right.

Effective organizations are doing the right thing when they research the market for customers' interests and needs and then provide the appropriate services or products. Effective bosses do the same. They analyze the interests and needs of their subordinates or co-workers and then adjust their management styles so that multicultural diversity is respected and valued.

Efficient organizations and bosses do things right. They constantly evaluate their management and supervision processes for strengths and weaknesses and make the appropriate changes. They not only gather data on how to offer services, market a product or manage a workforce, they are concerned with moral and ethical decisions and how these decisions can be made fairly in a multicultural organization.

Effectiveness and efficiency go hand in hand. Both are essential for good and better bosses. However, having an idea for a good program or product is not the same as implementing it. Implementation requires flexible leadership.

The effective boss is flexible enough to be able to change bossing styles whenever it seems appropriate. Doing this is part of "doing the right thing" instead of staying stuck in what doesn't work and is therefore wrong.

The efficient boss also shifts management styles in such a way that the employees involved will know that their boss is someone who cares about their well-being and who is doing things right.

Bosses who are leaders are both effective and efficient — and something much more. They are able to envision harmonious and well-working multicultural organizations and convey this vision to others. Regardless of their titles, these leaders are the better bosses.

Self-discovery

Most bosses use one or more of the styles listed on a regular basis. Think of several bosses you have had and the bossing skills they used most often. Rate them and yourself. Put marks on each line on the chart with a plus and minus for each style. Then connect the marks and observe the patterns.

The director:

demanding   discerning

— ————————————————————|———————————————————— **+**

The coach:

interfering   encouraging

— ————————————————————|———————————————————— **+**

The delegator:

neglecting   empowering

— ————————————————————|———————————————————— **+**

The analyst:

calculating   caring

— ————————————————————|———————————————————— **+**

The peacemaker:

appeasing   negotiating

— ————————————————————|———————————————————— **+**

The defender:

bullying   advocating

— ————————————————————|———————————————————— **+**

The innovator:

confusing   creating

— ————————————————————|———————————————————— **+**

Now look back at the above. What bossing styles do you use most often? How might you be rated by your boss? By your subordinates?

Would you get a different rating from those who are from a different race or ethnic background, different age, gender, or physical condition than you are? If so, why?

If you are having difficulty with a particular subordinate, would using a different bossing style help the situation? How could you start making the change?

So what to do

If you like your self-evaluation, just keep on doing what you're doing! It's evidently productive. Apparently you're already a good or better boss and helping others to realize their potentials.

However, if you see yourself in ways you don't like, then the easiest way to improve is to consciously practice using the positive sides of your bossing styles. Experiment for one week.

■ Write your memos and answer your phone from the plus side of your bossing skills. Say things such as, "I'm glad to hear from you," or "I think that's a good plan," or "I'm interested in hearing your ideas."

■ Be aware of using your bossing skills. For example, If you seem to be a Demanding Dictator, try actively listening to other people's ideas. Entertain the possibility that they might be right and see what happens.

■ If you tend to be an Neglecting Delegator, deliberately plan to walk through your department, greeting others with something like, "How is your work going?" "Do you have enough time to do it?" "Do you need help or do you think you can manage?"

Whenever you catch yourself bossing in a negative way, deliberately use the opposite form of the bossing skill you are then using. If that doesn't work, switch to another style.

Everyone has the capacity to be a Discerning Director, an Encouraging Coach, an Empowering Delegator, a Caring Analyzer, a Negotiating Peacemaker, a Determined Defender and a Creative Innovator. See what happens when you expand your bossing skills and approach others in different ways. You will probably find out that when you act like a good or better boss, employees will respond positively. The emotional climate will improve and motivation will increase.

2

The personality factor

How to understand personality

People can be understood, subordinates can be understood, and bosses can be understood using a theory called Transactional Analysis, often abbreviated to TA. The theory of T.A. was developed in the 1960's by psychiatrist Dr. Eric Berne (best known for his book, *Games People Play,*) and became more popular with the publication of *I'm Ok — You're Ok* by Tom Harris and *Born To Win* by Muriel James and Dorothy Jongeward. Since first developed, the theory of TA and its applications to organizational, educational, and clinical work have expanded worldwide.

TA has become popular because it is an extraordinarily useful tool that can be used to understand and enhance all of life. It is stimulating and practical. It can be applied immediately to both on-the-job and off-the-job situations. Even a basic knowledge of Transactional Analysis is helpful in learning how to improve communications and for understanding personality factors that affect both job and home relationships.

TA can be used to understand people in organizations of any
size, from a small family-owned business to the largest government agency or corporation. Its tenets apply to all people of
all cultures at all times so it is useful in a multicultural world.
The basic principals are so universal that it is currently being
studied in at least eighty-three countries, in universities and
other organizations.

Many professional organizations provide training in TA. When
people hear its principals they often respond, "Yes, that's
right. Now I understand." This response is common throughout the world, regardless of the culture or the language being
spoken.

All nations are multicultural but even nations such as the
United States and the Soviet Union which are primarily multicultural do not always appreciate cultural diversity. Often they
do not. Some are not aware of it, some are threatened by it,
and others notice it but don't know much about it and don't
know how to relate to people who are different from themselves in some way. Whether the cause is ignorance, fear or indifference, the fact is that attitudes about cultural diversity are
often related to personality factors.

Why people are the way they are

According to TA, everyone's personality is composed of three
parts — the Parent, the Adult, and the Child ego states. When
capitalized in this book, they refer to personality parts. When
not capitalized, they refer to specific persons.

An ego state is defined as a consistent pattern of feeling and
experience which is directly related to a corresponding pattern of behavior. Some of these patterns make for good habits
and some for habits that are not so good. All people often act
automatically, responding on the basis of habitual feelings and
behaviors that they developed in response to specific experiences. For example, people who in childhood have dogmatic

and restrictive parents often demonstrate a similar pattern without recognizing its source.

Whereas managers who habitually act like controlling parents were once acceptable in most cultures, now they are often resented by people of any race or national background who have learned to think and act independently. Women as well as men are also resenting overcontrolling bosses.

Yet this same bossing behavior may be more acceptable for those from Asian and Hispanic cultures where such behavior is more common in the family and carries over to the workplace.

When people, bosses or not, speak and act as their parent figures once did, they are functioning from the Parent ego state. Everyone has different parents and incorporates some of their specific attitudes and opinions into their personalities. Therefore, each person will be somewhat different when functioning from the Parent ego state. For example, one boss may feel positive toward employees of a particular racial or ethnic background, and another feel very disdainful of the same ones.

They are this way because the family culture in which one is raised usually affects personality development. It is in childhood that many people decide who they will like and trust and who they won't.

Children who grow up in multicultural situations and experience people of different races or ethnic backgrounds being kind to them, usually appreciate various cultures on the job.

However, those who grow up in situations where teachers or neighbors of other cultures are abusive, are likely to be suspicious of those particular cultural groups. Similarly, those who have opinionated parents or teachers are also likely to be suspicious. Later in life this can be very difficult because people often hang onto their childhood feelings, whether they are aware of doing so or not.

In many situations the cultural background of employees' parents shows in their personalities. In the United States there are many people who had grandparents who were slaves. These grandparents handed down stories of courage and stories of the humiliation and suffering under which they lived.

The reality of this fact, that slaves were cruelly bossed by many white owners, has resulted in many blacks, or African Americans, as many prefer to be called, feeling angry at whites or despairing about the possibility of receiving fair treatment from them.

Derrick Bell, Professor of Law at Harvard, believes that many of the laws designed to extend civil rights to blacks have benefitted many whites and that correcting injustices by law does not solve many of problems concerned with regulating the economic and political power between blacks and whites, because old prejudice remains.

On the other hand, when people, including bosses of any race or ethnic background, feel and act as they did in childhood, they are usually functioning from the Child ego state. The Child ego state includes very positive qualities such as friendliness, curiosity and creativity. It also includes the capacity for negative behavior. Manipulating with temper tantrums, controlling with bullying behavior or withdrawing out of fear are some of the many adaptations that are made in childhood because of training and trauma.

Each person has a unique combination of childhood experiences. So, when in the Child ego state, each person is unique. However, few people are entirely ruled by the feelings and decisions of their inner Child.

When bosses are thinking and acting rationally, when they are gathering facts, estimating probabilities and evaluating results, they are functioning from the Adult ego state. Using the Adult ego state does not mean that the decisions they make are right. They may have wrong information or lack pertinent details.

For example, some bosses who want to be good bosses may not be aware of laws against discrimination on the basis of race, gender, age or ethnic background and therefore do not support their employees in claiming their rights.

Other bosses may have full information about these laws and still be indifferent about abiding by them. As an example, Mei-Lie Ching functioned very efficiently as a computer programmer. When a coworker sexually harassed her, and she didn't know there were laws against it, she quit her job to get away. Her boss had been aware of what was going on but did not realize it was offensive enough to cost the company an effective employee. Replacing her with someone of like skills was costly and could have been avoided.

Using ego states

Most people, at one time or another, exhibit all three ego states. Rubin Miller was a supervisor and effective computer programmer who, from his Adult ego state, could write and run a 150-step program while his coworkers would still be wondering where to start.

Occasionally he overused his Parent ego state and was exceedingly sarcastic with his subordinates, just as his father had been with him. And, if very tired or frustrated, Rubin sometimes exploded in anger as he had done in childhood when he was frustrated.

In other words, Rubin Miller could act rationally from his Adult and irrationally from his Parent or Child. Coworkers who came from backgrounds where similar behavior was expressed usually shrugged off his sarcasm and tantrums. However, other programmers in the same office who came from more restrained family backgrounds were appalled and whispered to each other that he acted like a bully when he was angry.

All ego states are useful, depending on the situation. It is not always best to act only from the Adult ego state. Sometimes it is appropriate to act from the Parent or Child ego states.

When a friend is hurt, sick or worried, sympathy from the Parent is called for. Going to a party is more enjoyable if the fun-loving inner Child goes along. When analyzing a budget the Adult ego state needs to be in charge. With awareness, a good integration of the three ego states is possible. Ego states are diagrammed like this:

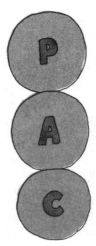

Diagram of Personality   Simplified Diagram

The Parent ego state

Each of the management skills and the poor or better ways they are used can be identified as coming from one of the ego states. When bosses direct others like dogmatic dictators, they are usually functioning from the Parent ego state. Like many parents they may strongly criticize those with less power, and use absolutes such as "always" and "never" and firm directives such as "you should" and "you must," while shaking an accusing finger at a subordinate.

Organizations of many kinds do that finger-shaking routine. Recently, in California, a debates was raised about what kind of ethnic language could be used on personalized license plates. The state had a committee that screens individual requests. One person of Italian descent insisted on using the word, "wop" on his license plate; another demanded the word, "dago." These words were considered to be ethnic slurs by a large Italian organization who protested to the licensing bureau. The decision has not yet been made but the case illustrates how two parent-type regulatory organizations can be caught in a double bind.

A different kind of directing can come from the Parent ego state of managers who are like discerning directors. They may also be firm and use a lot of "shoulds." However, their behavior is intended to help others, not control them negatively.

Nurturing parental behavior is demonstrated by both interfering advisors and encouraging coaches. They may pat others on the back encouragingly, look sympathetic, and say things such as "Don't worry, it'll be all right," or "Come on, I know you can do it."

The difference between bosses who are interfering and those who are encouraging coaches is that the interfering one automatically assumes that others will make mistakes and continually hovers over these employees. This overnurturing behavior is actually overcontrolling and often interferes with employees' personal growth. Encouraging coaches know that people not only need encouragement and approval, but also chances for trial and error so that they can development their own judgment.

This kind of behavior is often used by some hospital staffs who treat patients that do not speak English as if they are helpless children and incapable of understanding. Actually, many who do not speak English well can understand much that is spoken.

Neglectful delegators sometimes demonstrate a less common form of parental behavior. Their indifference is somewhat like that of mothers or fathers who are physically or emotionally absent.

Bosses like this are often accused of being cold and distant. In conversations, they tend to look away from others and show little facial expression, often seem preoccupied and may not follow up the assignments they give to others.

The empowering side of delegating bosses is that they liberate others. They stay somewhat distant yet make sincere though relatively brief contact with employees and empower them by giving them lots of freedom with comments such as "Do as you think best" or "The job is yours, just come to me if you get stuck." This is particularly effective when men give this freedom to women and women bosses do the same with men.

The Adult ego state

Bosses who use the positive side of any bossing style, whether they are directing, coaching, delegating, analyzing, peacemaking, defending or innovating, generally have strong Adult ego states.

However, the skill that is most commonly associated with the Adult ego state is analyzing. Bosses who are strong in this skill continually ask who, what, why, when, where, how and, especially, how much?

When analysis is used negatively, bosses analyze for the sake of analyzing, computing like non-feeling robots. They imagine that they are acting from the Adult ego state but do not recognize that people, as well as money, are important in every organization.

Better bosses whose major function is to analyze have integrated healthy parental concerns and child-like feelings and thus can give feedback and information with a humanistic concern for employees. They can respond as whole people to whole people.

Usually well informed on issues of equal opportunities and the value of multicultural diversity, they use their information to promote a healthy working climate. For example, they understand that employees may have strong feelings on how they are addressed. They learn things such as that most people from Brazil do not like being called either Latinos or Hispanics. Portuguese, not Spanish is their native tongue. To speak of them as South Americans is acceptable but they prefer to be identified by their country of origin, not by race or language.

As citizens of the United States, they tend to speak of themselves either as Brazilians or as Americans. However, they do not put the two words together as do some other racial, national or language groups.

The Child ego state

There are three typical childlike behaviors that often show in the Child ego state of grown-ups. These occur when a person is trying to make peace, or fighting to defend something, or struggling to create something new.

Appeasers are would-be peacemakers who often wheedle and manipulate others by looking helpless, woebegone or anxious. They try to please others but feel unable to do so. Instead they may constantly shift, squirm and act placating and apologetic out of a childhood fear of not being liked, or of being punished, or of being used or abused in some way. Such bosses are often trying to appease their bosses as well as their subordinates. They may not please anybody because they are so afraid of displeasing somebody.

Peacemakers who use the plus side of their peacemaking skills present a different picture. As children they were taught to "play fair" and they continue to do so on the job. They watch and listen carefully to others and seldom express strong feelings that can overpower others. Instead they say things such as "Let's think this over before making a hasty decision." They skillfully use the right words at the right time, and this keeps the doors open for further negotiation.

Bullying bosses are those who are hostile and misuse the skill of advocating. They constantly "go looking for something to fight about." They may taunt others like children who want revenge, and who provoke aggressive behavior in others.

This fighting type of personality, which is motivated by the rebellious part of the Child ego state, is more effective when used by someone who acts like an assertive advocate. This boss, who may also assume a fighting stance, is not basically hostile but enjoys challenging authorities with strong arguments.

When representing their employees to the administration, these bosses can be quite aggressive. However, they do not put others down. They simply stand strongly for what they believe in and often think of themselves as crusaders on the side of what is right. They often get involved in situations that require them to act as advocates and they do this willingly.

Innovators, when they are overusing the Child ego state, are sometimes scatterbrained. Scatterbrains are like hyperkinetic children. They are very active physically. Their attention span is short. They may pace their office, go rapidly from one person's desk to another, forget their agendas, look confused and flighty, and say such things as "You lost me," or "I thought I told you that."

The creative innovator is a better boss who also tends to be physically active, looks excited but not confused and can construct ideas that hang together instead of a jumble of ideas that go off in every direction. Like a precocious child, the creative innovator often breaks away from routine and arrives at new, workable ideas or different ways of looking at the same old problems. When creating new strategies, this boss also uses intuition and insight.

Switching ego states

All bosses use the Adult ego state when they think and act intelligently and rationally. Some prefer it and feel most comfortable when in the Adult. Others prefer using other parts of their personalities in conjunction with the Adult. A common mistake of many bosses and subordinates is to believe that they are always in their rational Adult ego state when such is not the case. They are often likely to be using some of their Parent or some of their Child.

One of the goals in TA is to learn to shift energy from one ego state to another at will. Some bosses do it well. Some do not. If bosses do not shift energy easily, it is because they have rigid ego state boundaries, or because the thinking of the Adult ego state is contaminated by the opinions of the Parent or the feelings of the Child.

Rigid ego state boundaries

Ego-state boundaries are normally like semi-permeable membranes and, depending upon the situation, psychic energy is supposed to be able to flow through them from one ego state to another. If the boundaries are too rigid, a person may appear to be quite inflexible or stuck in in some way because the power of each of the ego states is not being fully used.

The problem of rigid ego-state boundaries is found in people who use only one or two ego states but don't allow the other to be exposed. This is diagramed as:

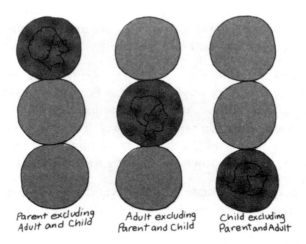

Parent excluding Adult and Child   Adult excluding Parent and Child   Child excluding Parent and Adult

Some people are in the Parent ego state most of the time. They often act parental — either negatively or positively — and thus may treat others as if they were children needing a critical or nurturing parent. Such behavior can be found in the secretary who always comes in early to "take care of everything" or in the manager who tries to run the personal lives of employees; and in the person who displays little curiosity, involvement, or sense of humor.

Either knowingly or unknowingly, these bosses sometimes choose others to associate with who are also strong in the Parent ego state. Together they may share the same opinions or prejudices. Other times these bosses select people who are constantly in the Child ego state and who like being dependent or like having a boss to complain about.

Whereas all bossing calls for analyzing from the Adult ego state, some bosses use only the Adult and exclude the Parent and Child. They are consistently objective and primarily concerned with facts. They tend to select jobs that are object-oriented rather than people-oriented, are prototypes of robots, and impatient with those who "bring their personal problems to work."

They tend to think abstractly in preference to responding forthrightly as a caring analyzer. This is ineffective with people. Calculating or machine-like behavior does not bring out the caring and creativity in others.

Some bosses function primarily from the Child ego state. As such, they may act very playful and create warm and friendly relations. Or they may act hostile and demanding like sulky children when things do not go their way. If they are innovators, they may constantly be dreaming up something new, adapting the ideas of others, or creating their own ideas.

Having such rigid ego state boundaries and being constantly in one ego state can be a problem because all ego states are valuable. Energy needs to flow back and forth between the healthy parts of the Parent, Adult, and Child.

In multicultural organizations the better bosses will be alert to new employees who may experience some form of culture shock when joining an organization. They will coach them through the adjustment period and respond to them in a friendly way.

Employee responses to bosses' ego states

The concept of a boss being bossy is often a holdover from childhood. Many children see parents as bossy and conclude that anyone in an authority position should or shouldn't act that way. When they grow up, these people tend to boss others as they themselves were bossed, or modify the parental behavior that they learned from their parents, or reject parental behavior entirely.

Many employees respond to bosses who constantly use the Parent ego state by gossiping behind their backs with resentful remarks such as "My boss is always telling me what to do," or "My boss is always hanging over my work and trying to give me help that I don't need and don't want," or "My boss never talks to me, so I don't know where I stand."

Other employees prefer bosses who substitute as parents and may say positive things such as "I may get criticized a lot, but at least I know what my boss wants," or "My boss is willing to help so I don't worry about little mistakes," or "My boss leaves me alone to do my own thing, and I like that."

Some employees perceive authorities as being mechanical computers, as data banks with bodies. They may resent this and complain, "All my boss knows is facts and figures."

If they perceive a fact-gathering boss as a caring analyzer, they may affirm, "My boss listens, understands, and gives me clear instructions."

Some employees view all authorities as belligerent bullies. They might like to beat them up but can't. On the other hand, some may see the positive side of a fighter style of boss, the side that is a strong defender and advocate of human rights.

When managers are appeasing peacemakers instead of strong negotiators, employees often respond with dismay or anger when negotiations to meet their needs are not successful. They perceive such a boss to be like a frightened child who tries to please whoever has the most power. For example, an employee may want to take a day off to celebrate a religious holiday, and the appeasing boss may not be strong enough to present this request to the manager. Another subordinate, especially one who comes from a culture where parents are very protective and involved with their children, may want time off to attend a special school function or to stay home with a sick child. If these issues are not negotiated in reasonable ways, then resentment usually builds up against the boss because the employee's values are discounted.

Creative bosses can be viewed by employees as impulsive and confusing or as interesting and exciting, depending on whether they act in OK or not-OK ways (which will be discusses more fully in the next chapter). Problems arise when these bosses are so inconsistent that they don't implement their creative ideas effectively. As a result, employees complain, "Things around here are always changing so fast you can't trust what tomorrow might bring," or "Why bother with today's objectives 'cause they'll be changed tomorrow before lunch."

Whether they are owners of companies, group project leaders or directors of government or non-profit agencies, creative innovators are often enjoyed by others. An employee might comment, "Although I don't always understand the big ideas coming from the think-tank, they sure keep things exciting around here."

Whatever style they use, bosses are seen by others in ways that reflect the three ego states. This may or may not be the way bosses see themselves.

Contamination of the Adult ego state

A very common mistake of many bosses is to believe they are thinking clearly when actually their thinking is contaminated by prejudices and fears. Contaminated thinking occurs when negative feelings left over from childhood and set opinions absorbed from parent figures seep through the Adult ego state boundaries and interfere with clear Adult thinking.

Everybody has some contamination, at least in some areas of their lives. It is most noticeable when people talk about how to rear children, spend money, engage in sexual intercourse, or be politically active. These subjects often arouse strong childhood feelings and parental opinions which are not based on current fact.

Contamination is diagrammed as:

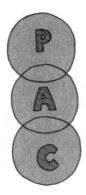

Common contaminations expressed on the job include opinions about how an organization "should" be run, how training "should" be conducted, the bossing style that "must" be used. It is especially prevalent in issues affected by cultural diversity. For example, employees with Hispanic or Japanese backgrounds usually expect to socialize a bit before meetings. Those with German or British backgrounds may expect to "get down to business" immediately and may be against any form of socialization.

When gender is a consideration, and it often is, there are many common contaminations. Men are often expected to move office furniture and carry heavy packages and suitcases even when their physicians advise against it. Women are often expected to fix the coffee, bring in the flowers and make things look pleasant. When individuals do not want to conform to these kinds of cultural expectations of their gender, they often draw criticism.

Even worse contaminations are that people of a different race, religion, or ethnic background, or older or younger people, or those in wheel chairs, or those who dress or speak in certain ways could not possibly be efficient managers. Such prejudices usually originate with opinionated parent figures who have become part of the Parent ego state. They are not based on current reality. In one large city bank, women tellers with European accents were considered charming by the manager who was European, whereas those with Asian accents were seldom hired.

Contamination of the Adult by the Child ego state is easy to spot. It shows, for example, when feelings of inadequacy lead to over-compliance, or when anger leads to bullying, or when fear leads to withdrawal.

Show-off behavior because of childlike delusions of grandeur are also contaminations because people tend to overvalue their own powers and importance. Some employees, fresh out of graduate school and with no experience, may feel "entitled" to make the same salary as experienced persons. A very smartly dressed boss may imagine a smart appearance to be a sign of obvious intelligence.

Conflicting values and contamination

Bosses who feel "entitled" to make all decisions are usually exaggerating the importance of their roles to the detriment of their clear thinking. This can obviously lead to conflict with others, or be experienced internally.

Internal conflict occurs because each ego state in a person may think and feel differently about a particular issue. For example, a manager who has a target date for a report and who also wants to take a four-day weekend vacation is likely to experience inner conflict in priorities. The inner Parent might demand "Work before you play." The Child might feel sulky and respond inwardly, "Yes, but I don't want to work." And the Adult might referee with "This project is due Friday." If the Child feelings of resentment are very strong, then they are likely to seep into the Adult ego state and costly mistakes may occur.

This contamination is diagramed as:

As another example, a personnel manager might be instructed to increase the number of employees who are women and members of a particular race or ethnic group who also have the potential for managing at upper levels in an organization. If prejudiced against women bosses in general or against people of a particular racial or ethnic background, this personnel manager may feel angry about the instructions, like a child who feels angry at having to obey authority instead of her own inclinations.

This anger can contaminate the selection process, lead to procrastination on the assigned task and the use of excuses: "No good candidates have applied; there don't seem to be any women available who have the right potentials for these management jobs."

When unaware of inner conflict, bosses often treat other employees with impatience. In a large packing company, many of the workers were refugees who did not speak or understand English well but were willing to work for minimum wages. The bosses didn't bother with the new law that encourages businesses to offer ten hours a week of basic education to such employees. They constantly talked about communication problems and did nothing to solve them. This was contamination from the Parent ego state.

The clearest way to recognize contamination is to consider whether or not objective facts are presented. If not, then communication is likely to be unclear. Behavior not quite appropriate to the situation occurs because the thinking is obstructed by Child feelings and Parent opinions. Naturally this interferes with effectiveness and efficiency.

Bosses who become aware of the punitiveness of some inner Parent opinions and inner Child desires, in themselves and in others, are on the way to becoming decontaminated, at least for that moment. Thus, their personalities will be more versatile and they will function as better bosses.

Effective and efficient personalities

At any time or place the use of one ego state rather than another may be most effective. Some employees seem to work best with a parental-type boss. Others respond more positively to a thoughtful adult-type boss. Still others prefer the boss who shows a lot of childlike behavior.

Effective and efficient ok bosses know that flexibility is an important key to success. They do the right thing by shifting energy from one ego state to another when shifts are appropriate. This is being both effective and efficient.

Even as each management skill has a positive side, so too has each ego state, and each can be used in OK ways. Good and better bosses recognize the continuing importance of this flexibility when responding to the increasing challenges in a multicultural world.

It is appropriate to use some nurturing Parent behavior if someone is injured or grieving, or some critical Parent response if someone is goofing up, or some more liberating Parent if someone is already performing well and offering to do more.

In a situation in which a contract is about to run out, it might be very appropriate to use Adult analyzing skills along with some powerful defending and peacemaking tactics motivated by the Child.

It's also appropriate to use the Adult as Executive inside yourself to decide when, where, how and with whom to use other parts of your personality. To become more aware of yourself and others and shift ego states or bossing styles in order to maximize potentials, are major signs of better bosses.

Self-discovery

Energy often shifts back and forth from one ego state to
another in people who are not "stuck" in a particular ego state.
When energy shifts, one ego state becomes more active than
others. In the past month when did you feel and act somewhat
like this?

Or like this.?

Or like this?

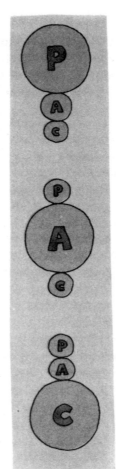

Think of a meeting you recently attended. How might you
draw an ego state portrait of yourself at that time? How might
you do this for two or three others who were also there?

Did you act differently to some people because of their race, gender, age, or some other form of cultural diversity?

- What kinds of cultures do you feel most comfortable with and which ones are hardest for you?

- How do you suppose you got that way? How has it affected you?

If you knew that a group of Japanese or Dutch or Argentinean managers, with the power to sign a contract that would benefit you, would visit your organization next week, would you do any special research such as going to the consulates or to libraries for materials that would help you understand their cultures? Would you expect them to understand yours? Why?

So what to do

Good bosses make mistakes but, in contrast to poor or mediocre bosses, they learn from their mistakes and don't keep making the same ones over and over again. Repeating the same mistake is usually because the reason for for the mistake is ignored or because the result of the mistake is not taken seriously.

Therefore, if you are having trouble with particular employees, for example, stop and think a minute, what might be the reason and the result? Do you withhold attention and give them indifferent treatment when they need information and encouragement? Do you nag like a critical or interfering parent? Are you, by any chance, a little hostile or overly appeasing or scatterbrained?

If so, you are probably using the wrong ego state for the situation or using the negative side of a bossing skill. Become more aware of people in your immediate environment.

Pay attention to body language. Are people looking down-cast? Do they have a far-away look and seem distant? Do their shoulders droop? Are they suddenly restless? Unpredictably slow?

Unreasonably belligerent? Or do they appear to be bored and looking for a challenge?

Pay attention to what they are saying. Is it something like, "I can't do this; I'm so confused by the instructions." "I'm doing my best; I think it's Max's fault." "I'm so worried I can hardly work today; my son has a 102° temperature."

How do they say it? Are they whining, belligerent, confident, insecure, nervous, excited? What ego state do they seem to favor? Under what circumstances do they shift ego states?

Next, based on the information you've gathered, consider your options. You could try another management style. If you use a Parent ego state and act like a discerning director instead of a dogmatic dictator, will others listen to you more often?

Other options might include: Apologies, if in order! Counting ten before exploding. Taking time to carefully explain a new program or procedure. Offering encouragement. Giving praise. Asking for opinions or information.

If you don't like the way others perceive you, what would you need to do differently? Do you need to learn more about the value of multiculturalism so that you can give more appropriate Parent critiqueing or encouragement and pertinent Adult information? Do you need to release your friendly Child and smile more often? If so, as an encouraging coach might say, "Go for it."

3

Psychological positions and better bosses

Ok and not-OK meetings

All managers have some measure of control over others and feel positive or negative about these people. With employees they consider to be their "own kind" they are often more comfortable than with those they do not understand because of ignorance of cultural differences or because of the psychological positions they have taken about members of particular cultural groups. Psychological positions are reflected in the choice of facilities and equipment, in hiring practices, in one-to- one encounters and in group meetings.

Consider a departmental meeting. Whether it is an informal brainstorming session or a more structured one the interactions, even before the meeting starts can be either positive or negative. Even psychological withdrawal is a form of interaction. There is often some positive and some negative interaction between those who attend or some psychological withdrawal while waiting for the meeting to begin.

Those who feel comfortable and confident tend to talk to each other easily. Those who do not feel this way may sit quietly as if lost in thought, or doodle on pieces of paper, or yawn and act sleepy.

The ways in which bosses and employees interact at times like this reflect their attitudes about themselves as being OK or not-OK. The various behaviors also reflect the attitudes individuals have about others being OK or not-OK.

In Transactional Analysis, the attitudes about OKness and not-OKness are called "psychological life positions" because they usually develop during childhood and may last for a lifetime. They are beliefs about oneself and others that are experienced internally and are expressed externally as typical behaviors.

The first psychological position is positive and is typical of good and better bosses. The other three are negative. Briefly these attitudes are:

> I am (we are) OK, you (they) are OK.
>
> I am (we are) OK, you (they) are not-OK.
>
> I am (we are) not-OK, you (they) are OK.
>
> I am (we are) not-OK, you (they) are not-OK.

People in the first position of I'm OK, you're OK are *effective and feel confident.* They have a "get along with people" attitude and take a positive, constructive approach toward others.

In group meetings they are willing to assume leadership but do not dominate the discussions because they value others' input. They use disagreement positively and keep meetings focused on the agenda, not on personal animosities. Because of a basic confidence in people, they can moderate emotional outbursts if they occur but generally head them off by keeping their meetings task-oriented.

Whether they are part of an ethnic group in power or not, confident managers tend to trust their employees and judge them by their performance, not their sex or color. While recognizing that many misunderstandings can arise because of cultural diversity, they make the most of opportunities to build and develop cooperation.

People in the second position of I'm OK but you're not-OK are *egotistical and feel superior.* They often act arrogant, condescending and paternalistic. This is a "get rid of people" attitude because their style drives people away.

In group meetings they lay down the agenda and do not encourage interruptions or disagreements which they assume would be useless. Others who attend such meetings are glad when they are over so that they can get away from such a boss.

The historical arrogance of white males over women and people of color is the clearest expression of this feeling of superiority. In cultures where socio- economic classes are considered to be important the attitude may show in paternalism or control.

People in the third position of I'm not-OK but you're OK are *anxious and feel insecure.* They have a "get away from people" attitude and often withdraw from others, act discouraged and compare themselves negatively with others.

In group meetings they try to avoid taking strong leadership roles, and may act laissez-faire, or defer to others who have been with the organization longer than they have or who might speak with more authority.

Historically, women have often perceived themselves to be in this position. Even today, few women have the courage to be free of such a strong cultural heritage. In meetings they may speak less than men and defer to them for important decisions or they may seize control and refuse to listen at all.

People in the fourth position of I'm not-OK and you're not-OK act *depressed and feel hopeless.* They have a "get nowhere with people" attitude. They often expect to fail and give up easily. Or they go plodding along paths of futility.

If they are leading group meetings, the meetings may become depressing as the leaders go nowhere, either in creative planning or in designing strategies to implement any kind of plan.

In meetings where young and old employees are meeting together, the experienced may write off the young as dreamers or fools, and the young may discount the old as too rigid to change. At the end of a meeting those who are considered to be too young or too old may feel hopeless about those at the opposite end of the spectrum.

Identifying OK and not-OK positions

The same psychological attitudes that are expressed in group meetings are also expressed between individuals. Take a billing situation for example. A boss who confronts a bookkeeper about not billing customers promptly may speak confidently, "I believe you can figure out a good procedure to use for this client."

On the other hand the same boss may be egotistical and boast, "Why is it I'm the only one around here who knows how to get things done!" A boss with an insecure position might complain, "I just can't get this billing to work out right. Probably you can." And the hopeless feeling boss might lament, "These books are a total mess. I give up!"

Confident, egotistical, insecure and hopeless bosses sometimes use similar words but their nonverbal messages may say something else. Attitudes of OKness and not-OKness show in gestures, facial expressions, posture, and other forms of body language.

An affectionate grin conveys a message of "I like you and I like me." A frown or sneer conveys quite the opposite. The tone of voice can also be a tip-off. Imagine how four different bosses might speak to an employee regarding a job description:

Confident boss: "Your job description is going to be changed somewhat. I'd like you to be satisfied with the changes before they are finally decided." The confident boss conveys the idea, "I respect you and will consider your ideas." (I'm OK, You're OK).

Egotistical boss: "Your job description has been changed while you were on vacation and don't forget who's boss around here!" The egotistical boss conveys the idea, "I'm in control, and you'll have to accept the job description whether you like it or not." (I'm OK, You're not-OK).

Insecure boss: "Your job description has been changed and I don't know what to do about it. Anyhow, you've been here longer than I have, so you probably have better ideas about it than I would have." The insecure boss conveys the idea, "I'm not adequate as I haven't written the description clearly and you could do it better anyway." (I'm not-OK, You are OK).

Hopeless boss: "Your job has been changed. The changes aren't all that good, but it probably won't matter anyway." The hopeless boss conveys the idea, "Nothing is any good, including the job description, and it wouldn't matter if it were." (I'm not-OK, You're not-OK).

The origin of psychological positions

When people feel confident they see themselves as capable of succeeding and interested in doing excellent work. They look for opportunities to improve their own skills and the skills of others because of a basic I'm OK and You're OK position.

When they do not have this double OK attitude, it is usually a result of their childhood interaction with their total environment of family, school and neighborhood. The negative attitudes developed in childhood are often carried into later life.

Children who are mistreated physically or emotionally at home, in school or in the neighborhood often conclude they are not-OK in some very basic way. Sometimes they think they should have been born the opposite sex or of a different race or ethnic background or even that they should not have been born at all. They imagine that if they had been different in some way they might have been loved and protected, or at least accepted.

The four basic psychological positions that show at work usually develop in childhood. Consider how a parent might ask a child to share in cleaning up.

Confident parent: "Last week you and I agreed that you would put your dirty clothes in the hamper when you take them off and before you watch TV. I believe you can keep that agreement."

Egotistical parent: "You never put things away when you're done with them. You're a slob just like your father's family."

Insecure parent: "I can't ever get you to turn off the TV. I guess I'm not a very good parent, but maybe you know best."

Hopeless parent: "The papers you hand in to your teachers are messy and so are you. But I give up; you never listen to me anyway."

Children who are reared by parents who feel and act egotistical, insecure, or hopeless may find it stressful in adulthood to be organized enough to get the job done. When asked to turn in a project on time, they may want to respond to their bosses as they didn't dare respond to their parents in the past. In contrast, when children are reared by confident parents who give them encouragement instead of condemnation, they usually grow up to feel confident on jobs that require turning in reports on time.

As another example of how psychological positions originate, some children who are handicapped or different in some way from others in the schools conclude they are not-OK. Other children may work doubly hard to overcome feelings of inadequacy. When they are older, either pattern may be expressed on the job. And many children who are attacked in school or in their neighborhoods may continue to expect physical or verbal attack at work.

Steven Ching's parents immigrated to the United States when he was seven years old to teach in a university where they had studied previously. Both spoke fluent English yet neither recognized the ridicule Steven suffered in school because he did not speak English. He finally learned it but the Child part of his personality was already injured by his early experiences.

However, when Steven grew up and was in his Parent ego state he felt I'm OK and you're OK, confident, much like his parents felt. However, sometimes when sick or under extreme stress he would go into the insecure feelings in his Child ego state and feel very anxious, especially if he was with people who could not understand any Chinese.

To those who had no understanding of his cultural trauma, Steven appeared somewhat rigid, even egotistical because of his formality and the fact that he seldom smiled. They did not know he had turned off his inner Child because of his fear of being ridiculed again.

When children are accepted and praised realistically they usually decide that they are OK and keep this attitude when they grow up. Whether bosses or subordinates, they will be the ones who do not make as many mistakes as others because their Adult ego state in not severely contaminated by the training and traumas of the past. Furthermore, when they do make errors, they seek to correct them promptly and move on to the next task.

Hiring practices of OK and not-OK bosses

Psychological positions can be observed in any area of responsibility, including hiring practices.

Confident bosses tend to seek out confident employees and encourage anxious and depressed employees to develop their fullest potential. They are not upset by the occasional person who acts superior and are able to delegate authority when it is appropriate.

Egotistical bosses overestimate their importance and affirm themselves by hiring inadequate or depressed employees so that they can feel superior to them. Sometimes the subordinates object to being in this position and try to gain control in one way or another. In response, the egotistical boss may repress them even further and aim to keep them there. Occasionally they get employees who fight against being kept down. These employees may act even more superior than their boss and may threaten to gain control in one way or another.

Insecure bosses feel inadequate in many ways and often attract those who act superior or arrogant and who are willing to tell them off. If they hire either confident or depressed employees, they often become more insecure because they are unable to please such people.

Hopeless bosses are those who have given up and "thrown in the towel." If they have egotistical employees, they feel even more hopeless and futile because they can't manage them well. If they have other depressed or hopeless employees, they feel trapped into endless futility.

Facilities, equipment, and OK bosses

Psychological positions are sometimes observable in the physical facilities and equipment that are supplied to employees. Although some bosses do not make decisions on budget control, and therefore have little power to change equipment, others do have some responsibility for these aspects of the job.

Confident bosses seek to provide a comfortable environment with good ventilation and temperature control for their employees, as well as for themselves, The working area is kept clean, often attractive. The furniture fits the bodies of those using it. The acoustics are planned so that neither bosses nor employees are fatigued by a constant barrage of noise. Lighting is given careful attention, and the lounge areas show warmth and creativity in their decor.

Egotistical bosses are more concerned over their own comfort, and sometimes the comfort of their customers, than that of their own employees. They may easily rationalize the acquisition of new furniture for themselves without awareness that their subordinates' furniture may be out-of-date, impractical or downright uncomfortable. Some egotistical bosses order large quantities of matching furniture at discount. Although the furniture may match and be pleasing to the eye, it may not be compatible with the personalities or bodies of those who use it. Egotistical bosses do not care. The company uniform chosen by such a boss can be a masterpiece of wrongness because the boss does not consider what employees might like to wear.

Insecure bosses are often depressed and may work in dingy holes, giving the "best" to others - other bosses, subordinates or customers. They negatively compare themselves with those whom they see as being more OK than they are. Furthermore, they may not care if the department also works in substandard, unattractive or inefficient surroundings. The secretaries may have to "make do" with poor equipment, the training department may be denied adequate training space, those with responsibility may have no power to implement it, and so forth.

Hopeless bosses, having given up, do nothing. They believe, after all, that they are not OK and neither are their bosses or subordinates, so why try? They also believe that neither their organization nor any other similar organization is OK, so it does not matter what the physical conditions are. They are just marking time waiting for the end and have no hope for something better. If their organization is bought out by another one that redecorates the office, hopeless bosses still find something to feel bad about - a window, a file cabinet, the air conditioner or coffee machine, the brand of computer or new style of administration will often be faulted by the manager who feels hopeless.

Employees' psychological positions

Employees respond to their bosses in ways that reflect their own psychological positions. They too may be confident, taking an I'm OK, you're OK position. Or they may express one of the three negative positions. For example, when job descriptions are rewritten because the organization takes on a new program or is being down-sized to cut costs, various responses from employees could be:

Confident employee: "Thanks for asking for my opinion. I have some ideas I think might be useful to both of us." (I'm OK, you're OK.)

Egotistical employee: "That job description won't do at all, and the union will back me up. Evidently, you haven't reviewed the contract." (I'm OK, you're not-OK.)

Insecure employee: "I don't know if I can do what you want but whatever you decide is probably right." (I'm not-OK, you're OK.)

Hopeless employee: "Yeah, I'll try to do the job but probably it won't work out, nothing ever does around here." (I'm not-OK, you're not-OK.)

These kinds of responses may be strong and direct as above or much more subtle. People of Japanese and Filipino cultures do not believe it is correct to speak up to their bosses. For anyone, if there job is at stake, the tendency is to be somewhat cautious in responding.

For example, in a shipping department if there is a rumor that some employees will be laid off, those who are packing merchandise are likely to be careful when complaining to a supervisor. The supervisor may be careful when complaining to a manager. Similarly, the manager may be cautious when going to an executive, and the executive may be cautious with a Board of Directors. Each may try to hide their anxiety as well as their negative psychological positions.

Employees' problems with multiple bosses

The good and better organizations are those that have confident I'm OK, you're OK bosses at every management level. The poorer organizations are those where hopeless bosses feel not-OK about themselves and not-OK about others. Many organizations have both and employees have to learn to cope with multiple management styles.

Some bosses are responsible for hiring; other bosses may be responsible for training, for planning and organizing, or for directing and appraising performance, and so forth. Each may choose certain types of employees, those whose personalities fit theirs. What may please one boss may not please another.

For the employee who has multiple bosses, it can be very difficult, especially if each boss uses a different bossing style. With the egotistical boss who acts like a dogmatic dictator, employees may feel forced to defer when they would rather express their anger. And with bosses who are overly protective some employees might do better if they learned how to fight to protect themselves and their rights.

Project coordinators and secretaries in typing pools often develop great skill in coping with the OK and not-OK psychological positions of multiple bosses and necessarily so.

Multiple bosses are such a challenge that employees can feel confused by conflicting instructions, feel like a juggler trying to keep all the oranges in the air at once or like a magician who wants to pull a rabbit out of a hat. Being able to juggle responsibilities and perform magic are sometimes survival skills needed by employees who cannot afford to quit and have no opportunity to be transferred to another division.

The nature of cultural prejudice

Prejudice is a form of egotism. It reflects an I'm OK you're not-OK position. It is very widespread and takes many forms. The most common prejudices are related to race, ethnic background, religion and gender and show up in remarks such as "Whites can't be trusted" or "Blacks can't be trusted" or "Be careful of those Oriental" or "Watch out for people with accents" or "You never know what a woman boss will do."

Such beliefs can be held with the rigidity of one who says, Don't bother me with the facts; my mind is made up.: or can just be based on misconceptions that are not held to be the one and only truth.

These messages come from those who affirm, "I've made up my mind so don't bother me with the facts," This is the attitude of many bosses and subordinates and usually due to misconceptions or prejudices. The difference is that misconceptions change in the face of new information. In contrast, prejudices seldom change, because new knowledge is rejected without thought.

The basic element of any cultural prejudice is hostility against a certain group of people. It can start with the rejection of one disliked individual and the dislike is then attached to an entire group. Or it can start with disliking a particular group; then any one of that group is also disliked.

Gordon Allport, in his classic book, *The Nature of Prejudice*, notes five levels of intensity that occur with prejudice. These are verbal rejection using slurs or derogatory words, avoidance at work or in social situations, discrimination which denies individuals or groups equality of treatment, physical attack whether planned or spontaneous, and extermination of individuals or specific groups.

Slurs and ethnic jokes: Matteo Molinari had been brought into the home office from a subsidiary in Italy because of his unusual ability to analyze the effectiveness of advertising in Europe. Although he was competent in four languages, when ethnic jokes and slurs were directed toward him, he felt unable to respond.

Only with the intervention of a boss who was aware of the need to sometimes defend employees who were treated with such prejudice was it possible for Matteo to finish his assignment for the company.

Avoidance: Sandra Martinez was a young, intelligent word processor in the legal department of a large corporation. However, she was avoided at coffee breaks and lunch time because of her Hispanic heritage and also because she was younger and more efficient than most of those in her department.

It took a strong coach-type boss to educate the rest of the staff about the value of multicultural diversity. They had assumed she would have nothing interesting to talk about or that she would not be interested in what they had to say so they avoided her.

Denial of equal opportunity: Howard Stein had grown up in New York City. When he was transferred to the midwest, trouble began because he was Jewish. He was avoided socially and when job openings arose, was denied opportunities to apply for them although he was fully qualified.

Physical attack: Jim Highwater was a Native American from Oklahoma who moved east to take advantage of a new teaching job. One late, dark night he was attacked in a parking lot and savagely beaten by men who threaten to kill him if he did not "go back to the reservation where he belonged."

Extermination: Leroy John was a African American who grew up in Minneapolis. He was a confident employee who did not anticipate the rage of some white racists when he moved south. Pulled out of bed in the middle of the night, he was shot to death because according to his racist attackers he was "too uppity."

All of these forms of prejudice can exist in small or large groups of people. Whether the group is part of a political party, a business corporation or a non-profit organization, there are slurs and avoidances, denial of equal opportunities, an increase in physical attacks and the deliberate extermination of millions of lives, or extermination by indifference and neglect as with those who are trapped because of starvation.

Prejudice in any form reflects on the impoverished minds of those who do not fight it and there is a large number of such minds.

Good bosses are alert to this possibility and intervene when it occurs. Better bosses do more. Although they recognize that information about the value of cultural diversity is an important factor, they also believe that objective knowledge is seldom enough. They believe that employees, at all levels, need to be personally aware of how they stereotype, generalize, and express prejudice and be challenged to change.

Generalizing from a few examples is a sign of ignorance. For example many people imagine that because Hispanics have a common language background that they are the same culturally. That is not true anymore than Irish and English are the same. Nor is it true that African Americans share the same cultural background. Furthermore, Asians are not all the same.

With Vietnamese refugees for example, it is estimated that at least 60 percent of those who are refugees in the United states speak at least some English. This means that many professional jobs could be open to them if that fact was appreciated. In contrast to other cultural groups they often mix business and social relations. If bosses who are not Vietnamese are unwilling to do this, they are perceived as cold and non-caring and the Vietnamese, well-known for loyalty to their organizations, declines.

Some organizations have yearly racial or ethnic celebrations such as the Cinco de Mayo and the Martin Luther King Day. Better bosses realize this is not sufficient; recognition and appreciation of cultural diversity needs to be on-going.

Better bosses also believe that when the self-esteem of employees rises, prejudices decrease. So this kind of boss, regardless of the bossing skill used, will focus on the positive expression of it and demonstrate, by words and actions, the fallacies of prejudicial beliefs and convey that giving up prejudices is in the best interest in favor of the whole human race.

Effective and efficient confident bosses

Not everyone is a self-starter. There are times when some people need to be criticized, need to have limits set, need to have demands made upon them. Confident bosses can do this while still conveying an "I'm OK and so are you" message.

There are also times when some people need to be encouraged, nurtured, cared for, forgiven for their mistakes and coached so that they do not repeat them. Many employees and volunteers do not receive enough of this kind of help. Confident bosses recognize it and put out the extra effort to coach effectively without conveying the attitude of "You're not-OK if you need coaching."

Sometimes employees need to be left alone, need to be given freedom to do some independent thinking. Some people with overcritical or overnurturing bosses, would function better if they had bosses who would delegate authority and responsibility and trust them to do their jobs without constant supervision. Because confident bosses generally feel OK about themselves and others, they give others this freedom in which to grow.

Occasionally, people need to be encouraged to fight for what they want. Or they may need to be pacified so that they stop fighting when it's not productive. Or they may need to be stimulated to get on with their creative OKness. Confident bosses allow this to happen.

Thus they are effective because they know that constructive criticism and emotional support may both be necessary. They also know efficiency increases in a confident "I'm OK, You're

OK" atmosphere and they do everything possible to bring it about.

They especially crusade against any form of prejudice, whether it shows in derogatory words, avoidance, discrimination, or physical attack. They are not passive bystanders because their ethics and their common sense move them to action.

They tune into nonverbal messages from their subordinates. They hear the nonverbal messages from their bosses. They become aware of their own nonverbal messages. They change, at least in themselves, what needs to be changed and discover that changing themselves for the better often elicits positive change in the psychological positions of others.

Self-discovery

Everyone experiences many bosses - parents, teachers, supervisors, managers, or administrators - who have some control over them. List several you have known and how their psychological positions showed in their bossing.

- Confident bosses I have known:

- Egotistical bosses I have known:

- Insecure bosses I have known:

- Hopeless bosses I have known:

What was your response to each of those bosses? When you think about these bosses, what feeling do you usually have about each of them? A "gut" feeling of anger or depression, appreciation and liking, or what?

By any chance, are you prejudiced in some way against your boss or subordinates? How does your prejudice show and what do you say to yourself to justify it?

Now, imagine some subordinates are talking about you. Would they say you are confident? Egotistical? Insecure? Hopeless? What might lead them to say this about you? Furthermore, how might your own boss define you?

Recall a recent meeting you attended. Were there overt or covert expressions of prejudice? Against you? Against others? How did it affect the meeting?

So what to do

If you feel not-OK about yourself or your participation in a recent meeting, then develop a list of possible things you might do the next time you are in that kind of meeting.

Maybe you need to take a more confident, "I'm OK, you're OK" attitude. Maybe you need to learn how to be more casual and friendly. Or talk less and empower others more. Or defend the rights of some of your employees. Or involve others in your creative projects.

Look around the working situation. If it's drab, then brighten it up. If you and others sit a lot in chairs that are uncomfortable, figure out how to get everyone more comfort.

Become aware of how prejudice may be expressed around your workplace. Is there anything that needs to be done that you might do? Want to do? Have the power to do? If so, don't hold back. Use all the "clout" you've got to change not-OK psychological positions to OK ones.

4

Bosses who stroke
and bosses who don't

OK and not-OK strokes

Everyone has problems. Some problems are new and
interesting, some are old and boring, some keep changing and
are frustrating. On the job, the problems may be due to lack of
equipment, lack of commitment, lack of knowledge, or lack of
skill. Problems are common and are worsened by the stress
which occurs for many reasons such as repetitive tasks, long
hours and continuous pressure to perform. Stress can also be
triggered or made worse by the absence of strokes or an over-
abundance of negative strokes.

The word "stroke" is a colloquial TA term. It refers to any form
of recognition such as the greeting "hello" or a gesture such as
a handshake. Strokes can be verbal or nonverbal, positive or
negative. A smile or handshake is a positive nonverbal stroke. A
frown or an abrupt turning away is a negative nonverbal stroke.
One of the basic forms of strokes on any job is greeting others
with their names, "Hi, Sean," or "Good morning, Kim." Most

people accept these as positive strokes but not everyone does. In some cultures first names imply a degree of intimacy that may not be appropriate at work.

The importance of names

Customary greetings in work and social situations vary from culture to culture. As Copeland and Griggs point out in their book, *Going International,* people from the United States often jump to the use of first names too quickly and offend others who prefer more distance and formality.

Even when the intent of using a person's name is to give positive recognition, the use of first names is interpreted by many Asians as intrusive, artificial, or as evidence of poor manners. Although such employees may try to adapt to the custom of the organization in which they work, the good or better boss who wants to give good or better strokes asks people of other cultures how they want to be addressed.

Using a surname or title correctly is one of the signs of an astute boss. Titles can be culturally very important, but they have to be used in the right way in certain situations. In Germany and Brazil, titles are used with last names. Yet in Spain and Portugal, titles are used along with first names.

Although many supervisors and managers do not travel internationally, they deal with people coming to the United States as visitors, immigrants or refugees who bring their cultures with them. They may try to blend in to the larger culture or may prefer to keep their own customs. When, for example, the ownership or management of a hotel changes, policies and training on how to deal with people of diverse cultures may also change. Implementing these changes can be crucial to a hotel's success.

A large hotel chain was having difficulty with a high turnover in the housekeeping department of one of their major hotels. It became clear that the manager was very prejudiced against some of the staff, when he complained loudly that their names were too hard to remember and pronounce.

Bosses who value cultural diversity respect differences. They learn how to pronounce unfamiliar names. They are sensitive to the possibility that their verbal greetings, though given with the best intentions, may be felt as negative strokes.

When race or ethnicity are not issues, the use of names often communicates an imbalance of power. Many bosses use first names for their subordinates but expect to be addressed with a title and their surname. The title may be as simple as Mr. or Dr., yet the implication is that bosses are to be treated more formally than others because of their superior positions.

Another issue about the importance of names is that some women no longer want the titles Miss or Mrs. to be used with their names. It identifies them as married or not married. As men are not so identified, many women consider the custom to be archaic and sexist. The title Ms. is becoming more common to avoid this kind of discrimination.

In a recent court case when a judge refused to address a woman attorney as Ms. and demanded that she use Mrs. or Miss, suit was threatened. The judge apologized and his apology was written into the court record. However, external compliance may not change an internal attitude that perpetuates a gender gap.

The importance of names extends beyond individuals. It is not unusual for organizations to change their names or to spin off subsidiaries with unique names. Recently a large Japanese bank in Yokohama changed its typically Japanese name radically by renaming itself "The Tomato Bank." This new name, along with a logo of a tomato, was placed on a large sign outside their bank building. Deposits quickly rose by over 30 percent.

No doubt the bank's creative and innovative bosses recognized that in a culture such as Japan, where land is limited and agriculture has a high priority, identifying with farm products was a wise move and an important and playful stroke to the farmers.

Stroking skills

One of the most important skills every boss needs is to know how and when to give people strokes that validate them. When people are validated they feel confident about themselves and others and consequently are more effective on the job.

An important form of stroking that may go unrecognized is respectful and open-minded listening to someone's ideas. Peter Drucher believes that too many bosses "think they are wonderful because they talk well. They don't realize that being wonderful with people means listening well."

Direct compliments are another form of strokes. But wanting validation in the form of compliments has a cultural dimension. Some people like to receive them publicly; others prefer them to be given in private and feel uncomfortable if they are singled out in front of others for individual strokes. As another distinction, Japanese employees with their traditional value of group harmony, prefer positive strokes to be given to their work group not to individuals.

Akiko Fukami, a highly competent manager in an insurance company, did not like it when she was singled out at an award luncheon for special recognition. She felt very embarrassed because to her, the credit belonged to the department as a whole, not to her as an individual.

All people need specific kinds of strokes. If they can't get positive ones, they sometimes go for negative ones without being aware of what they are doing. "Be careful what you're doing, you dumb ox!" is a negative stroke that may be given to someone who is often careless.

To many people, even negative strokes are better than being entirely ignored. Although they do not deliberately plan to get negative strokes, they often do something to provoke them. They may come late for work and use heavy traffic as an excuse. They may forget the importance of follow-through and use the excuse, "I'm too busy to get it all done." Or they may leave work early with the excuse of wanting to prepare a presentation for the next day at home where they will not be interrupted. They may frequently use the office phone for personal calls with the excuse of checking up on their children.

Although any of these excuses can be valid, bosses who are neither sympathetic nor empathetic will criticize those who make it a habit of finding excuses. "Your excuses are not believable," says a parental type manager. The analyst boss may say "This is the third time you've been late this week and that will have to go on your evaluation." "Don't bother me again with your dreary problems at home. I'm too busy with all the advertising I need to get out," might be a comment from a confused, scatterbrained innovator.

Conditional and unconditional strokes

All strokes are either conditional or unconditional. Unconditional strokes are words or behavior that convey the message, "I like you just because you're you, not for what you achieve." This kind of unconditional stroke is the kind all children need. It helps them develop a basic "I'm OK" position .

On the job, unconditional strokes are seldom given except between peers who might say to each other, "I really like working with you. It makes the job more pleasant."

Off the job, unconditional strokes can also be scarce, whether between spouses or friends. Yet everybody needs them and needs to figure out ways to get them.

In contrast to unconditional strokes are those that are conditional on performance. Conditional strokes can be given with words such as "If you work harder you might get a raise" or with some kind of body language that conveys conditional approval if... (you agree with me, placate me, obey me). These strokes are given only if subordinates meet the conditions that are deemed important by their bosses. They are like the proverbial carrot held out to a balky donkey and are often effective, but only briefly.

Bossing styles and stroking messages

The stroking skills of poor or mediocre bosses can be compared with bosses who are good or better. Better bosses know what to do and do it.

Discerning Directors expect excellence and usually stroke employees only conditionally until excellence does occur. This is their way of getting employees to perform well. Such a boss might say, "You can do it if you put more enthusiasm or more effort into your job." Or "This report will be fine if you work it over one more time." These kinds of strokes acknowledge the employees' potential for excellence.

Demanding Directors do not expect excellence. They expect employees to do poorly and frequently give negative verbal strokes. They may yell or make sarcastic remarks such as, "What's the matter, can't you do anything right?" Or they may imply the same thing nonverbally by frowning, sneering or pounding a desk. Their stroking patterns — verbal or nonverbal — carry messages of "Don't bother trying to think, you're too stupid, just obey my commands."

Encouraging Coaches use a positive bossing style to encourage those who act inadequate or confused or helpless, to learn to be more competent. They give strokes of emotional support. They help others until they become self-supporting. They convey the message, "I believe you're capable of doing it."

Interfering Coaches, using a not-OK style, give most of their attention to employees who act helpless or confused. After all, this meddler kind of boss needs inadequate people, and coaches them to be inadequate by acting overly involved and not encouraging them to take any responsibility. The real message that is hidden in their strokes is "You can't survive without my help."

Empowering Delegators' positive strokes are affirming and especially appreciated because they are so rare. The nonverbal underlying message is, "It's your job, so you make the decisions." Employees of this kind of rather distant boss may learn, out of sheer desperation, to compliment themselves or to seek out verbal strokes from other significant persons.

Neglecting Delegators' strokes are so random and off-hand and given with such indifference that they have little meaning and no power. Such bosses do not recognize the need other people have for specific words and gestures of recognition for their efforts. Consequently, the basic message behind any stoke they may give is "Don't come to me for attention."

Caring Analysts, using a positive style, often smile and speak briefly to co-workers they meet in the hall, parking lot or the water cooler. They respond to the nonverbal as well as to the verbal statements of their subordinates and bosses. If they discover a high turnover of personnel and low productivity, they consider whether the working conditions might be the cause. They may decide that the workplace is emotionally sterile and that employees are stroke-deprived and need more attention. By spending more time talking to them, they give the non-verbal message, "You're important to the organization and I hear you."

Unfeeling Analyst bosses seldom give positive strokes. They do not stop by employees' workplaces to compliment them on a task well done, or inquire about their health, or ask about how things are at home. Their statements and questions are typically around economic values. When they are ruthless, they try to exterminate others. "You are expendable," is their ill-disguised message.

Negotiating Peacemakers respect people's feelings and tend to give the kinds of positive strokes that facilitate negotiations.

They avoid conflict with remarks such as, "Let's see if we can solve the problem together." They convey the message "I think you are the kind of person that is willing to cooperate to resolve conflict."

Appeasing Peacemakers are often unsuccessful in negotiating any kind of conflict. They are too busy trying to please and appease others. Their strokes do not increase job effectiveness because they too anxious to think clearly about what kind of strokes to give. Such bosses may compliment employees for their appearance when it is praise for actual accomplishments that would improve performance. The message these bosses give out is "I know you're apt to be difficult, but I hope I can keep the lid on."

Advocating Defenders fight fairly. They fight for their subordinates, for their peers, and even for their bosses. Advocates are similar to older siblings who stand up for the rights of those who are not in power positions. Like coaches, they are often effective team builders. Now that health benefits are such an important part of many employment packages, it is often the advocate type of boss who goes to bat for employees with the message "I'm on your side and I'm willing to fight for you."

Bullying Defenders like to fight with others and tend to give strokes to others who are similarly hostile. Sometimes their advocacy and desire to fight gets out of control, and they become belligerent bullies who enjoy giving out negative strokes. They are like vengeful children who want to get even because the world doesn't treat them as they wish to be treated. Such a boss may slap a person hard on the back while saying sarcastically, "I doubt if you can match that quota." This kind of stroke provides negative recognition that clearly says "Want to fight about it?"

Creative Innovators often use strokes in very effective ways. Their verbal strokes may be full of enthusiasm, "Wow, great idea," which of course encourages further creativity as most people enjoy receiving these kinds of strokes. Other strokes may include recognizing creative employees with office parties or trophies or time off. Their nonverbal message is "I'm glad you're you — and that you're creative."

Confusing Innovators, in contrast, often act flighty and scatter-brained. They are so desperate to be creative that they don't think things through. They may get started on new projects and then change their minds time and time again. In their attempts to be creative geniuses, they often ignore employees' needs for strokes. Their message is "Stroke me 'cause I'm the one who thinks up all the new ideas."

The stress of bossing

The three most common complaints of middle managers are that they lack the authority they need to make necessary decisions, the information that higher executives have about the nature of the organization, and the lack of interpersonal support and feedback that they need from their bosses.

The lack of authority, information and interpersonal support for managers is often due to prejudices that are held by those in higher management or at executive levels. In multicultural organizations the prejudice is often expressed as social avoidance. Although avoidance may not occur at office parties, going out to lunch with someone who is physically handicapped or of a different race may be avoided. Consequently networks and support systems may not be established and managers, regardless of their race, or physical capacities may feel as if something important is missing — and it is.

Bosses who learn how to use positive stroking can reduce their own occupational stress as well as that of other employees because work always goes better when positive attention is given to persons as well as to the work they perform.

When bosses give negative strokes too frequently, or when the strokes they give are so heavy-handed that employees feel like they have been battered in some way, it is often because the bosses themselves have a stroke deficit.

Having a stroke deficit is similar to having a vitamin deficiency. Sleep patterns may become irregular, the immune system functions less effectively, and one's body or emotions begin to break down. Being a boss is stressful and sometimes managers and supervisors feel as if they have nothing left to give. They feel as if they are operating in the red and have few resources and little energy to draw on.

When stress levels rise, problems such as high blood pressure or coronary heart disease become more common. Job dissatisfaction, worry about potential unemployment, and depression also increase. Extensive research in stress by pioneer Hans Selye has brought this problem to the awareness of many organizations.

In his twenty-eight books and over one thousand articles written on the subject, he explained his discoveries about the bodily reactions of people in stress situations. Currently, good and better organizations are looking at such situations in a fresh light to try to discover more about the causes of management stress.

It is impossible to avoid all stress. There are always stressful situations — driving in commute traffic or being handed one more assignment that has to be done "right now." But the ability to respond positively and cope with stress, without increasing physical or emotional problems, is often related to organizational climate and the ways strokes are given and received.

Positive target strokes

There does not seem to be any particular kind of stroke, either verbal or nonverbal, that appeals to everyone. Warm and hearty handshakes are appreciated by Chinese men but not by the French or Arabians. A jocular air and big smiles that are meant to be friendly can be interpreted by the Japanese to mean that the subject under discussion is not deemed to be important.

While such generalities do not apply to everyone of a given race or ethnic background, they are like guideposts that point in a general direction and indicate that those from one culture or subculture have their preferences and those from other cultures have theirs.

Although it is impossible to know all these differences and respond to them, the better boss makes a conscious effort to give the right kind of positive strokes that correspond to cultural values. When this is done, these strokes become positive "target" strokes.

Target strokes are very specific strokes designed for particular persons and given for particular reasons. The best ones are carefully thought out and carefully executed. They can be given from any ego state and sent to any ego state. They really "hit the target" because they are what the other person hopes to hear.

Some target strokes are simple and unconditional such as a sudden "Hey, let's go to lunch together," or a sincere "You're fun to work with." Some strokes are conditional and given only for performance. Employees often look for both kinds of strokes.

Currently, more women are asking for strokes that recognize the rational thinking they use when in the Adult ego state. This is relatively new because the strokes traditionally given to women on the job have been more for their nurturing Parent who made the coffee, or for their compliant Child who would try to please everyone by doing the work that nobody else wanted to do.

In contrast, many men are looking for the kind of strokes that until recently have been primarily given to women. Men are recognizing that they are nurturing and may want paternity leave to share in the care of a new baby. They may want recognition for the Child part of their personalities that may, for instance, love nature and motivate the Adult to work to protect the natural environment.

Yet each person's stroke needs are different. Take a department problem with absenteeism, for example. One manager
may want a stroke for Adult rational thinking and may get it
when his boss says, "I'm glad you gave me those figures on absenteeism for your department. Now I understand some of
your supervisory problems more clearly. " A different employee might prefer sympathetic strokes to the inner Child, "You
really worked very hard to get those figures for me."

Still another might hope for a "wow" stroke that comes from a
boss's inner Child and get it with, "Wow, you really do have a
problem with absenteeism. The figures show you have a really
tough problem. You'll just have to `hang in there' and it ain't
going to be easy."

To complicate it a bit more, in any one person each of the
three ego states may want different strokes. Tom, Dick, and
Sherry are examples:

Some people are aware of their stroke needs, some are not.
Furthermore, people's stroke needs change from time to time.

The strokes they want one day may not be the same as what they want the following day.

Negative target strokes

Positive strokes increase loyalty and productivity; negative ones reduce both because they are designed to hurt or make others feel inadequate in some way.

A sneering remark such as, "You couldn't sell anything important if you tried," would at best alienate people who already doubt their selling abilities. At worst, it could send them into a spiral of depression and discourage them from learning how to be successful.

Many ethnic, racial or gender jokes are thin veils for negative target strokes. Ridicule or sarcasm are the same, though more direct. Teasing and joking is not customary in many cultures and any kind of barb which is given from an egotistical position can only reflect negatively on the one giving it. This includes comments such as "That's a pretty good presentation for a woman!" or "Not bad, for a kid like you!"

Such remarks can be aimed at a target in such a way that they eventually backfire. Those who make such remarks may begin to wonder why people avoid them. "After all," the joker may say, "I'm just trying to be friendly. What's the matter with everyone? Can't they take a joke?"

Effective and efficient stroking

Some bosses automatically, and without thinking, spray generalized compliments around carelessly hoping that some will be effective. They seldom are. Good or better bosses using the OK side of bossing styles focus their strokes for maximum benefit.

They know that everyone needs strokes and that some people need more strokes of a certain kind than others. Without these particular strokes, they tend to shrivel up in some way. Their work may go sour, their ideas may become less creative, they may be absent more often, and their errors and poor decisions may increase. Though competent and well paid, they may move to other organizations that give positive strokes more generously.

Good bosses become better ones when they use positive target strokes with appreciation for cultural diversity. These strokes enhance feelings of self-worth. Good bosses also become better ones when they figure out what strokes they need for themselves and what they can do to get them.

Self-discovery

Make a list of five subordinates or bosses that you interacted with in the past week. After their names jot down the kinds of strokes you gave.

- Were your strokes conditional or unconditional?

- From which of your ego states did they come?

- To what ego state in the other person did they go?

- Did they hit the target in positive ways?

Now think about the strokes you received from others this week:

- What kind were they? If negative, how did you respond?

- If they were positive, how did they affect you?

Consider the stress you experienced on your job this past month.

- Was it created by others or by yourself?

- Was it related to strokes?

- Did it have anything to do with cultural diversity including race, national origin, gender or sexual preference?

- What about differences in work styles, in socio-economic backgrounds, appearance, health and any other variables you dislike in others or they might dislike in you.

So what to do

Regardless of the bossing style that has been used, regardless of the not-OK psychological positions and the negative stroke patterns that have been demonstrated, change is possible.

You can decide to operate from your own positive bossing style rather than your negative one.

You can decide to interact with others as a good or better boss who gives and takes strokes of confidence that imply, "I'm OK and you're OK."

You can plan to use some positive strokes that will hit the target. There are several ways to discover the target. One is to carefully observe what seems to turn another person on. What kind of action or remark from you adds bounce to that person's walk, or lights up their face or eyes, or results in renewed enthusiasm for the job?

Another way is to ask a straight question such as, "What positive comment would you like to hear from me?"

A third way to discover the target is with the use of imagination, intuition and two chairs. This method would not be appropriate in a busy work situation. It could be experimented with when you're alone. You may feel a little uncomfortable when you first try it but don't let that hold you back.

The method is to sit in one chair, get relaxed and imagine the other person in a chair close by and facing you. Start a dialogue. Say what you want to say. Then switch chairs and be the other person responding positively or negatively to your stroke. Continue the dialogue while switching chairs back and forth until the transaction feels completed.

Naturally, bosses need and want strokes too. How about you? Who do you want strokes from? Your boss? Your peers? Your subordinates? What kind of conditional strokes do you want for what you do on the job? What kind of unconditional ones would you like and from whom?

Look in your mirror and talk to yourself. Ask yourself what you want and need. Try the double chairs technique. Put yourself in one and imagine your boss or a peer or subordinate in the other. Start the dialogue to bring your stroke needs into awareness.

As another technique, go back into your memory bank where your childhood experiences are stored. Recall once more some of the target strokes you got then, or wanted to get. These actual or wished-for strokes are what you may still be wanting.

If you feel uncomfortable asking someone for strokes, then spend some time thinking about the question, "What's the worst thing that could happen if I ask for what I want?" The answer may be surprising.

A basic TA premise is that people are basically OK and will respond in OK ways if their stroking needs are met. However, many things happen to people so that they may stop feeling and acting positively. Good and better bosses recognize the fact and start out by discarding some of the negative characteristics of their bossing styles.

5

Transactional bossing

The exchange process

Much of life and work involves an exchange process. The
exchange can be payment for work performed, prestige for
work performed, or pleasure for work performed. However,
work is more than products and performances. In very important ways work involves continuous exchanges with people —
face to face, over the phone, through written memos and letters, telemonitors, video and TV.

In TA these exchanges are called transactions thus the name of
the theory. In any transaction, each person gains something
from the exchange. What they gain can be positive or negative,
and what they give can be either, depending on what bossing
style they are using, from which ego state each person is acting,
and what kind of psychological transactions are going on between them.

There are three types of transactions: complementary, crossed,
and ulterior. In every transaction, there is at least one stimulus,

a stroke that is either verbal or nonverbal, positive or negative, and one response which is also a stroke.

Complementary transactions

When a boss walks into a meeting and announces a bonus and those who are there respond with "Great news!" that's a complementary transaction because the news given, which is the stimulus, receives the expected response.

A less pleasing transaction is when the boss announces a cut back in federal funding and those who hear the announcement groan. However, this too is a complementary transaction because the groan is the expected response.

In complementary transactions the lines of communication between the ego states of the people involved are parallel and are diagramed like this:

When two Japanese women bow to each other on meeting or when two French greet each other with a social kiss, their transactions are complementary.

Bossing styles in conjunction with ego state transactions are often fairly obvious. A traditional example is of a dictator type of boss speaking from the Parent ego state and yelling, "Why can't you ever do anything right!" and an apologetic employee responding from the Child, "I'm sorry, I'm sorry, I'm sorry."

An analytical district manager might ask in a matter-of-fact voice, "Where are the sales figures for the month?" And the supervisor might hand them over, also in a matter-of-fact way. This would be an Adult-to-Adult complementary transaction. A Child-to-Child ego state transaction would occur if a hostile boss interacted with an equally hostile employee. A bouquet of flowers given to celebrate a big sale could also be from the friendly Child in one person to the happy Child in another.

And when a couple of "good ol' boys" sit around jawing about the "good ol' days" and about how things were or ought to be, it is their Parent ego states sharing opinions. Or when two employees lament about how their children are doing in school where teachers scorn their accents, that can also be the internal Parents talking to each other.

Complementary transactions are initiated not only by bosses. They also are initiated by subordinates. An employee may ask to leave the job early and expect a critical or nurturing parental response and get it. Or an employee may present a draft for a new program and expect, and receive, clear Adult feedback. In any case, as long as the lines between ego states are parallel, communication is open and can continue indefinitely.

However, even with open communication, complementary transactions are not always useful. When one person talks on and on at a meeting that has a tight agenda, a response of courteous interest would be less useful than a skillfully crossed transaction to stop the monologue. Knowing how to interrupt and cross a transaction is an important managerial skill.

Crossed transactions

Whenever a response to a stimulus is not what is expected, the transaction is said to be crossed. This occurs if the greeting "Hi, Harriet" gets a critical response such as, "Don't you see I'm busy?" or a plaintive response such as, "Please don't ask me how I am." When he gets such a response, Bill is likely to feel crossed up somehow.

In a crossed transaction, the lines between the ego states are crossed and communication is interrupted. When this happens, and it frequently does, people feel misunderstood, surprised, angry, confused, or sometimes relieved.

For example, when discussing a departmental budget item with a manager, a supervisor may be surprised if the boss cuts off the conversation with a brisk, "Don't worry about it." The same employee is likely to feel relieved if, after a prolonged discussion of the employee's failings, the boss suddenly crosses the transaction by shifting attention to something else.

Common crossed transactions are diagramed as:

When the not-OK side of a bossing style is used, crossed transactions lower morale, production and services. A shy employee approaching a manager with a useful idea for how to implement a project may be unwilling to make such an overture again if greeted with "Can't you see I'm busy!"

When bosses make a habit of crossing transactions, they deaden the enthusiasm of others who may become indifferent or despairing and say something like, "I don't make the decisions. I only work here," or "No matter what I say, nobody around here listens."

However, crossing a transaction is sometimes useful, especially with difficult people. For example, if a co-worker talks on and on indefinitely, a boss might interrupt with, "Yes, we've discussed that point already." Or to change the subject, if an employee sounds confused, overgeneralizes or babbles jargon, a good boss might cross the transaction with, "Is there something else you'd like to say but haven't quite formulated it?" Or, "I think it would speed up our decision if you outline your proposal first." Or, "Is this something important that needs correction? If so, what do you think needs to be done?"

From their OK sides, bosses often use crossed transactions as management tools to help themselves and others to work more efficiently, especially with difficult people.

Ulterior transactions

A crossed transaction often carries an unspoken message which contains a hidden agenda. These hidden agendas are ulterior transactions because the surface Adult-to-Adult transaction only partially hides a different message. A "Hello Sophia" given with either a wink or a sneer is an ulterior transaction.

Ulterior transactions are more complex than complementary or crossed transactions. The person who initiates an ulterior transaction uses two ego states at the same time and often hooks two ego states in the receiver.

When ulterior transactions are diagrammed, the words spoken are called the social transaction and are diagramed with a solid line. The ulterior message is the psychological transaction and is diagramed with a dotted line. Common ulterior transactions are:

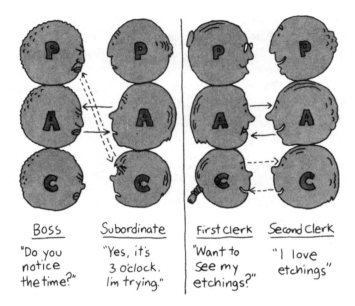

Boss	Subordinate	First Clerk	Second Clerk
"Do you notice the time?"	"Yes, it's 3 o'clock. I'm trying."	"Want to see my etchings?"	"I love etchings"

At the social level, the Adult ego state in the above transactions seems to be doing the talking. Actually, it is one of the other ego states that is sending the vital message, the psychological message.

Ulterior messages are given in many ways. Some ulterior messages are given nonverbally with body language. It is not unusual for bosses to pound on a desk for emphasis, leave the room abruptly in the middle of a conversation, or give someone a pat on the shoulder.

Even clothes can carry an ulterior message. A boss that wears jeans to work is giving a message about informality. Someone who wears a high-necked lace dress is giving a very different message. In either case, the ulterior message is clear without a word being spoken.

Ulterior messages are also given with facial expressions as when someone winks seductively, or wrinkles their nose in distaste, or raise an eyebrows to imply doubt, or frowns disapprovingly. Various gestures meant to be pleasing can be interpreted in negative ways in different cultures. Gesturing with hands is appropriate in talking with Italians and South Americans but much less with those from England or Asia.

Arnold Farthing thought that looking people in the eye was a important way to establish rapport. However, some Japanese employees thought that when he did this he was disapproving of something they were doing and they considered it to be very disrespectful if they looked at their bosses directly.

The tone of voice also communicates ulterior messages. As any child might say to an authority figure, "It's not what you say, it's the way that you say it!" Whether it is a boss or a subordinate, when somebody plaintively whines, subtly ridicules or loudly attacks, powerful messages are conveyed. What the tone of voice conveys is often more important than the words.

People pick up ulterior messages because of the Adult ego state's powers of observation and interpretation, and the intuitive ability of the inner Child. Creative ability, also present in every Child ego state, is what is used to design the ulterior messages.

Sometimes ulterior transactions are more acceptable than those that are open and direct. If a student or employee is being sexually harassed, keeping physical distance from the harasser may be more effective than a verbal "Oh, don't."

From a manager, a frown may work better with some employees than leaving the room abruptly. Pacing the floor and looking worried may be more effective than an explosive "Can't you ever be on time?" A big smile for a job well done might be preferred to an engulfing hug.

The value assigned to a specific transaction depends upon the goals of the supervisor, manager, or organization as a whole. The goal of one boss might be to develop teamwork and effectively use coaching transactions calling for complementary responses from subordinates who agree with this boss. Another goal might be to gain information by mutually respectful Adult-to-Adult complementary transactions.

A less positive goal which is sometimes used in organizations with little heart is to get rid of tenured employees in such a way that the organization will not be responsible for their retirement or severance pay. To get these employees to quit, some bosses act like dictators or bullies to drive them out. They deliberately cross transactions with implied threats which are the basic messages or they give out strong ulterior messages that are even more threatening.

Computerized thinking

This is the age of the computer and the increasing use of computers at home and in a busy offices is changing the climate of many organizations. Well-known for his book *Future Shock* which was forecasting future trends, Alvin Toffler is saying that "in the past the world was divided by East and West, North and South. In the future it will be divided into the fast and slow. He believes that power will be defined as the ability of one person to quickly transmit knowledge to another.

In some high-tech corporations any employee can send messages via computer to the top bosses and bosses can do the same with employees. Many face-to-face meetings are being discarded in favor of networking through computers.

This can be particularly pleasing to those who are highly verbal with words and sentence structure. It can be distressing to those who are not. Although working with sophisticated computers is intellectually stimulating, it is not an adequate substitute for human interaction. As a result some people become stroke deprived. Looking at words or even graphics on a screen can interfere with the appreciation of cultural diversity and all it implies in terms of appearance.

Stephen Hawking, a great theoretical physicist who is severely disabled is, according to some, intellectually superior to Einstein. Unable to take care of any of his physical needs, or speak without his voice synthesizer and his one-finger-operated computer, he is forced to work out all his theories in his mind.

Imagine the kind of transactions he would receive in most organizations, from bosses or subordinates.

For him, the computer is necessary and does not interfere with the use of his mind. Yet, Theodore Roszak in his book *The Cult of Information*, speaks of the worship of the computer and the reality that "Garbage In" often becomes "Gospel Out," meaning that because something comes out of a computer many people believe it as if it was "The Gospel Truth." A strong advocate of thinking rather than depending upon pre-programmed information and misinformation, Roszak has elicited a number of negative strokes and discounts because he advocates using the computer as a *tool* for the mind instead of a substitute for the mind.

An increasing number of consultants and consulting firms are making themselves available to organizations that are beginning to recognize some of the issues of race, gender, age, and ethnic background that have been ignored for so long. Psychiatrist Price Cobbs, an African American who coauthored the classic *Black Rage* and currently consults with corporations on managing cultural diversity, points to the need for black managers to have mentors so that they can function in white corporate structure, that gays and lesbians may need opportunities to discuss ways in which they are discriminated against, and that many Asians will need help with their accents so that they can be more easily understood. These issues are increasingly calling organizations into accountability.

Discount transactions

In Transactional Analysis, "discounting" is a process that belittles the importance of people's problems and their ability to solve them. When bosses are discounting themselves, they are denying or ignoring their own feelings, thoughts, opinions or achievements. When they are discounting others, they use the same denial process. This can create so much stress that emotional, physical or job-related problems are accentuated.

For over two hundred years racial problems in the United States have been greatly discounted by the majority of white bosses who have either ignored the inequality of power or fought to maintain it. Because of deep prejudice they have not wanted to give equal recognition to African Americans and especially have not wanted to be in subordinate roles. This problem remains unsolved.

All too often problems that need solving are not solved. They are discounted through the use of denial. There are four common ways this is done:

The first way of discounting is to *deny the problem exists.* Some bosses ignore obvious departmental dissatisfaction which is obvious in lower productivity and increasing personnel turnover. Or they may ignore symptoms of individual employees such as alcoholism, depression, confusion, procrastination or fatigue. Or they may discount their own personal problems and focus only on the problems of others. In particular, they may discount their physical and emotional needs for rest and recreation and drive themselves until they collapse.

The second type of discount is to *deny the importance of the problem.* Bosses might observe an increased number of errors or increased absenteeism or increased friction between employees yet say that such problems are not important. Bosses may also deny the importance of their own problems and say, "Yes I'm very tired, but it's not that important as I'm so strong."

The third type of discount is to *deny that there is a solution* to the problem. An example of this is when a contract is lost because a culturally insensitive letter was sent and the boss prematurely concludes "You just can't work with those people!" This is particularly serious in organizations involved in international relations. If political leaders believe that world problems are really too complex to solve, their inertia can lead to the destruction of the environment, to severe economic sanctions or to all-out war.

The fourth type of discount is to *deny personal responsibility*. A boss may admit there is a problem but does not try to solve it. "Yes," a CEO might say, "we do have a problem with not having enough energy but you could hardly expect an oil company to be concerned over developing alternative forms of energy. Anyway that's not my job; my job is to sell oil."

Or a personnel manager might defend a position with "Sure we may not have many women in executive positions, but I can't find any good women candidates. All the applicants were hopeless. They have to be a certain style to fit our organization."

Obvious sarcasm or so-called "friendly" bantering are frequent on-the-job discounts that carry the message, "You're not-OK, as a person."

Complaining frequently about one's own inadequacies is a form of self-discounting that carries the message, "I'm not OK, and I'm helpless to do anything about it."

Poor and mediocre bosses use many discounts. However, good and better bosses do not. They do not ignore problems nor minimize their importance. Nor do they deny that there are solutions to problems, nor that they are personally responsible for helping to find solutions. They know that subordinates' opinions and feelings, as well as their capacities for rational thinking, are part and parcel of offering services and getting out products.

Managing difficult people

The definition of what constitutes a difficult person depends upon the one who is doing the defining. Bosses whose jobs primarily call upon them to direct others perceive the most difficult employees to be those who procrastinate or do not want anyone telling them what to do.

The coach type finds that the hardest to manage are those who think they know it all and resist any kind of help, or those who refuse to be part of a team.

To the analytical boss, confused or spontaneous-acting, creative employees are frequently the most difficult to manage. The reverse is also true. To innovative bosses, the rigid, compulsive and overly-structured employee is likely to be seen as difficult.

To the peacemaker, the fighters and challengers are the most difficult to manage. And, of course, the boss who really wants to fight is put off by the one who wants to negotiate.

However, in spite of these particularities there seem to be certain kinds of behavior that most frequently interfere with growth and harmony regardless of bossing skills.

Power-seeking is one of these. It is easily observable in those who try to dominate others and ignore their wishes. Power-seekers often talk on and on about a favorite cause or a certain product, program or procedure. In meetings they want to control the decisions and have the first and last word on whatever interests them. Managing them is relatively possible if they are first given some recognition and then the subject is firmly changed.

Herman Gunther a mechanic had a lot to say about the auto shop and much of it was valid. But he often went on and on, repeating what he had said before. This was difficult for others to listen to, so his boss experimented with different ways of interrupting. When subtle efforts failed, the boss interrupted Herman with a recognition stroke and then changed the subject, "Mr. Gunther, that's an interesting point you have made. Now that our attention has been drawn to that problem, let us move on to the next one."

Another kind of difficult person is the one who is an attention-seeker. Although it is normal to want attention, these people are so extremely self-centered that in meetings they will yawn or wiggle to show boredom whenever they are not center stage.

They also interrupt the flow of conversation with attention-getting personal anecdotes or innumerable questions or statements.

In meetings the attention-seeker can be managed by briefly giving them positive attention such as, "I believe Ms. Smith has something she would like to say. Can we hear from her now?" After allowing the attention-seeker to take the center stage briefly, the good or better boss can then take over the meeting again with, "Thank you very much for your comments. Now let us return to our agenda."

Sympathy-seeking people can also be difficult to manage. Whereas most people need and deserve sympathy at times of stress or crisis, those who constantly seek it slow down progress and interfere with decision making. By dwelling on irrelevant issues from home or minor criticisms at work, they solicit others to take care of them.

Tom Lee was like that. He was often late for departmental meetings and complained about being overworked at the ticket counter of an airline. He was even overheard complaining to customers. To intervene with his sympathy-seeking, his boss commented, "Yes Mr. Lee, you do indeed have a stressful job. In fact most of us do. Therefore, to start today's training session, let's all have a bit of fun and reduce some stress. Let's all turn to someone sitting close by and do a little complaining for two or three minutes."

After recognizing the reality of stress that often accompanies customer relations, the group functioned with more cohesion and with fewer irrelevant interruptions.

Transactions of effective and efficient bosses

The ways bosses transact with others often reflect the positive and negative poles of their bossing styles, their favorite ego states, and the psychological positions they have taken.

OK bosses recognize the value of clear, direct communication and, whenever possible, use complementary transactions. However, sometimes they deliberately cross a transaction or use ulterior messages to get their points across when a more open statement might not be acceptable to the other person.

Complementary, crossed, and ulterior transactions each have value. Communication can be closed off if appropriate or can be opened up if it needs to be.

Knowing the value of good communication with people of all cultures is one of the signs of an effective boss. Knowing how and when to use each kind of transaction is a sign of an efficient boss. Not discounting themselves or others, even when the others are difficult people, is characteristic of better bosses.

Self-discovery

Think back on transactions you've had in the last 24 hours.

- Jot down two complementary transactions. What were the results?

- Jot down two crossed transactions that you initiated or re-sponded to.

- Jot down two ulterior transactions that you experienced. What happened next and how did you feel?
Now think back and see if there were discounts involved.

Think of several different people with whom you work. What are the most common transactions with each of them? Who does what to whom?

Think of some persons whose race, gender, ethnicity or physi-cal or emotional health differs from yours.

- Are they from war-torn situations and still recovering from the crisis?

- Do they seem to be suffering from culture shock because the management style in your organization is so different from what they have known previously?

- Is there a tendency to discount their problems or the impor-tance of the problems they face?

So what to do

Be as honest as you can be with yourself. Changing a style of transacting is not always easy. Familiar ways of bossing often seem "right" to the person who is using those ways whether they seem right or not. Other employees resist change too be-cause they have become accustomed to Saul "just the way he is" or to Maria "always acting that way." If Saul or Maria does something different, some employees may feel confused or hostile or even glad.

So what to do? One thing is to admit that maybe your transactions are not always OK. Of course you probably do fine when things are going well. If you are like most other people, it's harder when the pressure's on. You may need to mend some fences and apologize to someone, or you may need to listen longer to someone before responding. Or you may need to assert yourself more.

Consider the organizational climate, morale, and production in your division. Is it high or low? Does it have anything to do with valuing or devaluing cultural diversity?

Look at your recent letters or interoffice memos. Analyze from which ego state the stimulus was sent. To which ego state was the letter or memo directed? Was it effective? Why or why not? Now see if the memo might be rewritten to reflect a good or better boss transacting with someone who might still be experiencing culture shock or discrimination in some form.

Skillful transacting can do much to raise productivity by raising individual and departmental self-esteem. When cultural diversity is appreciated, energy is released for more effective work and there is abundant energy left over to appreciate one another.

6

Psychological games at work

Games people play

Everyone plays psychological games, from entry level employees just out of school, to first-line supervisors just beginning to move up the organizational ladder, to managers at all levels. Even directors and CEO's have their games.

Games involve two or more players who play three basic roles: Victim, Rescuer and Persecutor. In this chapter, when the words victim, rescuer and persecutor are capitalized, they are referring to these roles. When they are not capitalized they refer to authentic responses to real-life situations.

Some people are actually victimized; others imagine they are, and play the role of Victim. Some people are bona fide rescuers; others imagine they are and play the role of Rescuer when they are not needed for that purpose. Some people are even legitimate persecutors. Many more people imagine they are entitled to be Persecutors even without the benefit of the law. Psychological games begin when somebody *unnecessarily* begins to play a role of Persecutor, Rescuer or Victim and in so doing "invites" others to play.

Switches between the game roles of Victim, Persecutor, and Rescuer are diagramed with arrows as on triangle below. The arrows indicate the way roles can switch.

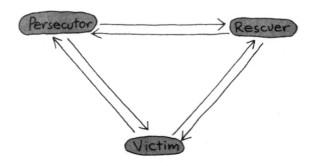

The roles are diagramed this way because people who feel like Victims often seek others who will act as Persecutors and give them a psychological kick. They are not aware of doing this and may, in fact, complain to themselves, "Why does this always happen to me?"

Supervisors may respond to a request for information by playing the game *I'm Only Trying To Help*. They leap in as Rescuers when asked simple questions. If their help is refused, they may switch to the Victim role and inwardly complain, "She asked me what to do and then turned down all my suggestions; I was only trying to help. Now I'll have to stay late and finish up her work and that's not fair."

The next day when the same employee comes to work the supervisor may still be resentful and play a Persecutor game of *Blemish* which is to find a little something wrong with everything the employee does.

Or, if playing a game of *Now I've Got You* the supervisor may act as a Persecutor, yell at an employee and then, when the employee works less efficiently, feels guilty for exploding, and may switch into a Victim position saying, "Oh, no matter what I do, it turns out wrong."

Or an employee feeling like a Victim may ask for help in negotiating a conflict with a co-worker. Then, when too much advice is given, the Victim may angrily reject it and turn Persecutor with "Stop telling me what to do all the time."

Victims often seek others to act as Rescuers and help them out, over and over and over again. After a number of efforts to be helpful so that the Victim can feel better, the Rescuer may begin to feel used and victimized.

Jose Lopez sincerely wanted to help other Hispanics get ahead in the agency in which he worked. Yet he often overdid his help. He took a strong paternalistic air with new employees and advised them about their work, their family and social lives, and even what clothes to wear, in spite of the fact that they often told him that they did not need so much advice. When Joe persisted, he was playing some kind of a psychological game — acting as a Rescuer when it wasn't useful.

When his help was turned down, he would sometimes sulk like a Victim hurt by other's lack of appreciation. Sometimes, Joe would not take on a Victim role. He would switch and become a Persecutor and strongly criticize persons who turned down his help. Occasionally he recognized his pattern and instead of switching into either role would stop the game and recognize that employees could think for themselves.

Game theory

In TA theory, a game is a sequence of transactions which, on the surface, appear to be a straight-forward series of complementary transactions. However, they are actually a series of ulterior transactions with specific hidden agendas that lead to negative feelings for one or both persons at the end of a game.

People who play psychological games seldom are aware of it. A person who constantly looks sad and often elicits sympathy from others is likely to play a game of *Poor Me, Look How Hard I'm Trying* and not even be aware of looking like a Victim.

This game is a favorite at all organizational levels. Those who start the game may feel self-righteous when hinting for help and say to themselves, "After all, look how hard I've been working." Or they may feel sad and depressed and, expecting no one to come to their rescue, say to themselves, "I know no one cares enough to help me out."

As in card games or games of sports, it takes two or more to play. If one person initiates a game by using an ulterior transaction that conveys, "Poor me, I'm a victim," this player could "hook" two different kinds of players into a game. One is a person who will act helpful and take a Rescuer position; the other is one who will act critical from the Persecutor position.

When things go wrong, as they often do in psychological games, the players are likely to think of themselves either as blameless for the unpleasantness or as unappreciated for their good intentions. They are aware that something unexpected has happened and feel as they have been tricked in someway.

The name of the game

Every game has a theme which can be recognized by observing what keeps happening over and over again that leaves one or more persons feeling or acting in negative ways. This theme becomes a colloquial term for the name of the game.

For example, a secretary who asks the boss to sign an important letter that has several typing errors is playing the game of *Kick Me*. In this game the secretary acts in a way that invites criticism and attracts others into the game who are willing to be critical and give a verbal kick.

The secretary's ulterior message is "Kick Me for my carelessness." The boss's ulterior message can be, " What's the matter with you anyway? Can't you do anything right?" Then the secretary feels inadequate and like a Victim once more from the position, "I'm not-OK, so its OK that you kick me." And the boss feels frustrated and takes the position "You're not-OK, so it's OK that I gave you a kick." Thus, at the end of a game one player feels inadequate and the other selfrighteous and both of them believe justice has been done.

A salesman who is continually late for appointments with customers and blames the traffic is playing *If It Weren't For Them.*

The purpose of the game is to avoid taking responsibility by putting the blame on someone else.

A boss who continually takes on more and more responsibilities, says "yes" to all demands, comes in early and works late, and sometimes works even at lunch-time or on weekends is playing the game of *Harried.*

Harried is being overly busy, then collapsing with depression, a bad back, ulcers, or a heart attack. The Harried player often leaves things in a mess for others to straighten out, feeling overburdened and self-righteous while doing so.

Other common on-the-job games are *Cornered* with the theme, "Damned if I do and damned if I don't"; *Uproar* with the theme "You stupid clod, you never do anything right;" and *Let's You and Them Fight* with the theme of one person stirring up a fight among others to prove once more that *"People are fools."*

Games are repetitive. They happen over and over to the same people in similar ways. There are innumerable games and it is not necessary to know all of their names. What is useful is being able to recognize the theme of a game.

The origin of games

Psychological games, like other games, are learned in childhood. Children learn them by imitating others or by taking the "roles" that others expect them to play. It is common for children to see their parents as critical Persecutors and nurturing Rescuers and to see themselves as poor little Victims.

Parents who continually persecute their children are like demanding dictators playing *Now I've Got You, You S.O.B.,* which is waiting for something to go wrong and then pouncing on the Victim.

When grown up, the children of persecuting parents often copy them, imitate their games, and act as demanding dictators or as belligerent bullies on the job.

Other children of persecuting parents become victims. They may act as Rescuers and try to make peace on the job as they once tried to do with their own parents. This may become their bossing style and they may remain very uncomfortable with any form of conflict and criticism. These people may play games such as *Look How Hard I'm Trying* or *Poor Me.*

Still other persons with similar punitive childhood experiences may block out their feelings entirely and go through life analyzing statistics without ever learning to care for those involved.

Parents who continually rescue their children in the manner of over-nurturing caretakers play games such as *Why Don't You,* which is giving too much "constructive" advice, and *I'm Only Trying to Help,* which is always being available and giving more helpful advice. On the job, grown-up children with this kind of experience may imitate their parents and become interfering coaches.

When children resent their smothering coach-type parents, they may act out creatively in many ways, or get very confused and anxious about making autonomous decisions.

Parents who are discerning directors or motivating coaches or competent delegators of responsibilities encourage their children to think analytically, fight fairly and cooperate creatively. People who are fortunate enough to have parents like this play fewer games than the rest of the human race. When they do play them, they do so less intensely, so the games are less destructive. These people are often classified as good or better bosses.

The game formula

Players are seldom aware of playing psychological games and awareness can be increased by recognizing the game formula, which can be used to understand the process of any game. The formula is:

$$C + G \longrightarrow R \longrightarrow S \longrightarrow X \longrightarrow P$$

C is the con that player #1 uses to get someone to join a game.

G is the gimmick of #2 player who has a weakness of some kind such as fear, greed, sentimentality or irritability, and can be "hooked" into responding.

R is the response made by #2 after being hooked into the game.

S is the underhanded and unexpected switch that player #1 then makes to trick player #2.

X occurs when player #2 feels confused or crossed up because of the switch.

P is for the payoffs each player collects at the end of the game.

Getting the payoff

In TA the feelings that are collected at the end of a game are payoffs. They may not be positive feelings but they are familiar ones that are used to justify the behaviors that follow. The feelings and behaviors are very much like ones that people had in childhood when things went wrong.

When people save up enough negative feelings they often feel entitled to some kind of payoff.

The angry person may feel justified in yelling and pounding a desk. The explosion is the payoff. It is often what the person has really wanted to do for some time.

The envious person may feel justified in gossiping and undermining someone else. The purpose is to put someone down in order to feel superior.

The depressed person may feel justified in making serious mistakes. The purpose is to get fired or get help before it is too late.

The fearful person may feel justified in doing nothing. The purpose is to avoid responsibility.

The self-righteous person may feel justified in being overly critical. The purpose is self-aggrandizement.

Strangely enough, many people are relieved after feeling bad and then acting out their feelings. But people around them often feel quite the opposite and may initiate a new series of games that are even more intense.

Intensity of games

Games are played at three levels of intensity depending upon how deeply the players are involved. They may be played with relatively mild commitment or may be played with life-and-death consequences.

First-degree games involve small collections of bad feelings and games that end like this are played in every work and social situation. They are not disastrous. The persons involved, with only a small collection of negative feelings, cash them in for a small payoff, such as a crying spell, a temper tantrum, going off a diet for a day or two, and so forth.

Geraldine Scott was a competent analytic boss who, because of studying for four years in England, had developed a British accent. It was thought to be charming by everyone except Chandra Kadambi, whose parents had come from India and resented British rule.

Chandra respected Geraldine as a manager and was puzzled that she did not like her personally. She was not aware of her prejudice against Geraldine because of her accent. Geraldine, sensed Chandra's ambivalence and acted increasingly indifferent and distant to her. In social situations, even around the coffee machine, the two women avoided talking to each other and when they did, they unknowingly exaggerated their accents.

It was not until they took a two-day training course on Transactional Analysis that they were able to recognize that they were involved in a game that had low intensity but was unpleasant. Both played the same game of *"Look How Smart (or Sophisticated) I Am."*

Second-degree game players have more invested in their feelings and in justifying their behavior. The collections they save and the payoffs they get are larger. The payoffs are often something the game player would prefer others not to know about, such as the development of emotional problems, or causing a car accident, or getting into serious financial difficulties. Sometimes the payoff for second-degree games is a "quit" of some kind.

People may quit school, quit an important relationship, even quit a good job. They justify the quitting because they've "been trying so hard," "taken too much," and are "sick and tired of being bossed around all the time."

Third-degree game players "go for broke." They play games as if their lives depended upon the outcome. They have huge collections of negative feelings because they have saved them up for years and years. Consequently, they go for the "big" prizes — homicide or suicide. Like frenzied, hysterical spectators at the end of the world championship games in soccer, they may run over others and kill them, or kill themselves in despair.

Organizations sometimes play third-degree games but in different ways. They kill off employees with overwork; they kill their companies with bad investments and lack of quality control. They also kill off other organizations with hostile takeovers. Big game players gamble for high stakes and often lose.

Big game players

At an organizational level second- and third-degree games can be played by employees who recognize situations of injustice but do not want to "get involved" by reporting them. The name of the game is *I Don't Know What's Going On.*

This game is also played in organizations when employees or bosses are caught for some form of carelessness or dishonesty. Others are questioned and may, if it is a serious game, claim the Fifth Amendment which is that no one is required to give evidence that might be self-incriminating.

At an international level, government agencies and the majority of citizens of an entire nation may say they didn't have enough facts to make a decision. They claim to be innocent due to lack of knowledge. Currently this game is being played out in relation to many issues that involve the natural environment or situations of famine, war and disease. Millions of people play *I Don't Know What's Going On* to defend themselves against doing something they know they should do.

The game is a serious one when citizens do not want to take responsibility for something important that needs to be changed. Later, when something goes wrong, they blame the legislature, administration or the court. Thus they absolve themselves from guilt feelings over refusing to act personally as advocates.

Defense industries that overcharge the government for what they manufacture, financial institutions that invest funds improperly, real estate firms that take money for what doesn't exist, monopolies that are illegal and find ways to evade the law are only a few of the many organizations that play seriously the *I Don't Know What's Going On* game. While the hoped-for payoff is lots of money, the actual payoff can be the loss of contracts or bankruptcy and perhaps imprisonment.

Businesses are not the only organizations that play games. Nonprofit humanitarian organizations sometimes use money that is donated for a specific cause to support a different cause. Religious organizations sometimes use donated funds to support opulent life-styles for a few of their leaders. Educational institutions sometimes use money in ways that do not encourage excellent teaching.

I Don't Know What's Going On is a game that often leads to disaster, whether it is an oil spill due to negligence or wasted tax revenues due to fraud.

The Rapo game

Every game, whether organizational or individual, starts with some kind of a "con." Some people are really con experts. If another person is "hooked" by the con, the game is on.

For example, the game of Rapo is often learned in childhood when a family member or neighbor acts seductively. It is often played in the office when one person offers an obvious sexual invitation by acting very flirtatious, wearing sexually provocative clothes, or saying something like, "Wouldn't you like to come up and see my etchings some time?" These kinds of hints are transactions from the Child ego state of one person to the Child in another. If the second player responds and makes a sexual overture, then the game is on.

Not all sexual encounters are Rapo games but when they are the initiator switches ego states and, like an indignant parent, criticizes the second player for responding to the con. This second player is likely to feel a moment of confusion and may respond angrily like a child who has been promised something and then let down.

Finally, as the series of transactions comes to a finish, each player in the game experiences an old familiar feeling such as self-righteousness, anger, sadness, guilt, or confusion.

These feelings lead to payoffs. Because of the feelings, each player feels justified in reacting in specific ways. Each "cashes in" their feelings in some way such as sulking, ridiculing, exploding, spending money they can't afford, or getting drunk while saying to themselves something like, "See, they're all alike. You can't trust any of them."

The Blemish game

Another very common management game is *Blemish* in which a parental type of boss insists that everything be absolutely perfect. The game can begin with a remark such as, "I'm going to detail all the things I want you to do, so pay very close attention." If said in a demanding voice, the other person is likely to take it as an order to be perfect.

The game continues if the second player responds to the order by trying very hard and then making one minor mistake. The first player, often feeling self-righteous, then points out this "blemish" and the second player may then feel depressed, explode in anger or tears, or defensively claim, "I'm not a machine. I'm just human. I can't help it if I make a little mistake once in a while."

Games are repetitive. People tend to play the same ones over and over again and may recognize the fact and remark, "Seems to me, we've been through this hassle before."

Interlocking games

It takes two or more to play a game and commonly one person's game interlocks with a complementary game of someone else.

The interlocking games of *Why Don't You* played by one person, and *Yes, But* played by another is an example: one player gives too much advice from a Rescuer position and the second player asks for it like a Victim and then switches to become the Persecutor. The interlocking games go like this:

Employee (cons by looking helpless): "I have a problem..."

Boss (hooked into responding helpfully): "Why don't you try..."

Employee (rejecting help): "Yes, but that won't work because..."

Boss (still trying): "Well, why don't you. . ."

Employee (still rejecting help): "Yes, but. . ."

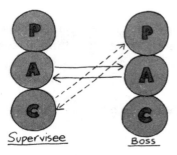

Finally the employee pulls an unexpected switch, which is the heart of a game, and denies the need for help. The *Why Don't You* boss gives up, feeling confused then frustrated, because the help was rejected. "Some people! You just can't please them."

At the same time, the *Yes, But* player feels a secret sense of glee. Once more an authority figure has been conned into trying to satisfy, and then put down because "None of the suggestions were any good anyway."

Games of effective and efficient bosses

Bosses who use the positive side of their bossing styles are alert to their own games and stop initiating them. When caught in a game initiated by others, they stop playing Rescuer — helping those who don't want help. They stop playing Persecutor — criticizing those who don't improve with it. They stop playing Victim — acting helpless and dependent when actually able to solve their own problems.

Bosses who use the OK side of any management skill may sometimes play games but the games are infrequent and usually only at the first-degree level. They know that authenticity beats game playing. They know that being straight-forward is better than being devious, that using the positive side of their bossing style is better than using the negative side; it is more effective and more efficient.

Self-discovery

Being able to stop games, or to lower the intensity of "hard" games into "soft" games that are less destructive are signs of OKness.

There is a procedure, a "game plan," that can be used to understand the process of any game that is played. To discover the plan the following questions are asked:

■ What keeps happening over and over again on the job that results in someone feeling bad?

■ How does it start?

■ What happens next? And next?

■ How does it all end?

■ How does each person feel when it ends?

■ What does each one do?

If one or both persons have negative or self-righteous feelings or behavior after a repetitive series of transactions, a game has been played.

There is, for example, the game plan of *Tricky Switches*, which is played by scatter-brain bosses and leads to employee resentment. The game starts when a boss continually changes procedures without reason.

The game continues with employees muttering something like, "Day after day she keeps changing her mind. First I feel confused because it happens over and over again. Then I feel mad. One of these days I'm going to quit." The quit is the end of the game which might have been avoided if the employee had not tried so hard to appease the boss and instead had fought for some stability or continuity.

So what to do

Bosses who want to stop initiating their own games, who want to stop getting hooked into other people's games, or who want to intervene in games between co-workers need to understand clearly the game theory, game plans, game roles, and game payoffs.

They need to be able to interrupt their habitual games and avoid interlocking with the games other people play.

To do this, an uncontaminated Adult is necessary. Therefore, Ask yourself, what is your weak point that someone can use to "hook" you into a game? Or in other words, what are you a sucker for? Is it worth the bad feelings you get after you've been had?

For example, if you get hooked into playing *Yes, But* your role is giving "helpful" advice. So the *Yes, But* game is stopped if you don't give advice. You can bounce the problem back to the person who presented it with something like, "What do you think would work?" or "I don't know what kind of help I can give you," or "If you take a little time, you can probably figure out the best way to solve your problem."

If you get hooked into a game with a critical dictator who plays *Now I've Got You, You S.O.B.* one way to break it up is to say something neutral like, "I'll think about it," or "That's an interesting point you made."

If you get hooked into a game with an over-nurturing coach who plays *I'm Only Trying To Help You,* you could say something like, "I prefer to do this myself," or "You're supervising me too closely. Please give me some space."

If hooked into a game with an indifferent delegator who plays *Don't Bother Me,* you could say something like, "I need some guidelines; are you willing to spend 15 minutes with me on this?" or "I haven't the authority to make this decision. Can we talk it over?"

If hooked into a game with a belligerent bully who wants to get a fight going in a three-handed game of *Let's You and Them Fight,* you could say something like, "I prefer not to hear the gossip," or "If there's something you don't like about that person, handle it directly, not through me."

If hooked into a game with a appeasing peacemaker who plays *Let's All Just Give In* you could retort, "I'd prefer not to fight, but we need to get some clarification," or "I've noticed that when we're honest we often solve problems."

If hooked into a game with a scatterbrained innovator who plays, *Let's Try It Twenty Other Ways,* you could say something like, "Would you sit down and explain the process slowly?" or "What are the variables that need to be thought through before we start?"

You can break up any game if you are willing to give up exaggerating your own strengths and weaknesses, and exploiting those of others. The simplest way to do this is to value the several cultures that are part of your personality and recognize that people of other cultures are also of value.

7

Scripts bosses live by

The global stage

Everyone has a psychological "script," a life plan that is much like a theatrical script calling for an on-stage production. As Shakespeare said, "All the world's a stage." People tend to live by their scripts without realizing what they are doing. The psychological games people play are short scenes in the life-long plays that are subplots in the vast drama that is taking place on the global stage.

Eric Berne said a person in a script is like someone at a player piano, acting as though he or she created the music and sometimes rising to take a bow or a boo from friends and relatives who also believe that they are hearing the "player's" own tune.

Scripts are pre-programmed ongoing productions that can be watched, much like T.V. serials. They dictate where people are going with their lives, what the action will be, and who else will be involved.

In addition to having different scripts, people play them out on different stages. It is not unusual for people to use one script at home and another at work. A script may call for being very efficient in the office and very inefficient in the kitchen. It may call for being docile on the job and like a tiger with a spouse, or just the opposite.

There are many kinds of scripts and many stages. Better bosses are becoming more aware of the global stage and the implications of being constantly connected with the whole world by computer networks and Fax machines as well as by phone, TV and mail. Although high-tech connects people, it does not necessarily lead to multicultural understanding.

Culturally diverse scripts in organizations dictate how "characters" are supposed to be and act. Sometimes personal scripts are not compatible with organizational ones.

Joseph Hall and Mitsuye Orr both worked in a magazine publishing firm. When it was bought out, Joseph was very dissatisfied and complained to her, "I used to like coming to work because it was so unpredictable. Even if the company did seem to be falling apart and I never knew what would happen next, it was lively. Since we've been bought out, things are a little too rigid for me. I feel as if I'm just playing a role, filling a slot instead of being me."

"That's what I like best about the buy-out," responded Mitsuye. "I like the predictability. It gives me a sense of family that I really miss. The old management was always changing procedures and never said why. Frankly I don't thrive on chaos. I prefer harmony and stability."

Clearly Mitsuye's and Joseph's personal scripts were quite different. Mitsuye's was compatible with the new organizational script so adapting to the new management would be easy for her and not for Joseph who preferred a more free-wheeling workplace.

One of the major changes that management is facing on the global stage is the openness with which people are expressing their sexual preference. In some organizations lesbians and gays are avoided or harassed; in other organizations sexual preference is sometimes accepted as a private choice. Currently there is a movement in large city governments, to give health and other standard benefits to all sexual partners of the same sex who are registered as living together.

Types of scripts

Even as all individuals have scripts, so do cultures and subcultures. Even departments within an organization are scripted. The types of scripts that people use as their life plans are the destructive scripts of losers, the banal scripts of non-winners who go nowhere, or the constructive scripts of winners.

Destructive scripts can be both self-destructive and destructive of others. Individuals or organizations with destructive scripts eventually lose. They may lose gradually, over an extended period of time, or with dramatic suddenness.

At a personal level destructive scripts may show gradually in the use of alcohol or drugs that lead to deterioration of faculties, or may emerge suddenly with the final curtain being a bottle of pills, a stabbing or a gunshot.

Destructive organizational scripts include those that demand more than is reasonable. They are often perpetuated by bosses who use the negative sides of bossing skills and whose psychological positions reflect a management attitude of "Those people aren't good for much." Sometimes destructive scripts come from the top bosses whose apathy and indifference allows destructive people, programs or services to continue in an organization when they need to be terminated.

Bosses with destructive scripts expect "the show" to collapse and, knowingly or unknowingly, contribute to it. When this is the case, the health of their employees may deteriorate gradually due to an overemphasis on productivity that creates excessive stress and sometimes leads to early death.

Organizations with destructive scripts are often indifferent to the suffering of others. They do not feel responsible for tragedy that may occur at many levels. They are either hostile toward employees or exploit them. Destructive organizations may also participate in illegal dumping of toxic wastes that destroy the environment, the unlawful discrimination against some people in the organization, or the illegal exploitation of people from "Third World" countries, stockholders or clients.

Banal scripts are scripts of non-winners. Neither destructive nor constructive, these people merely go nowhere. They avoid change. They restrict their own growth, limit their own opportunities, and are not interested in developing their full potentials. They usually live bland, routine lives with little sense of meaning or mission.

On the surface they may appear to have constructive scripts (after all, nothing really bad seems to happen). But they do not accomplish much because they do not establish clear goals nor do they establish procedures for reaching the goals they do have. Like squirrels in cages, or the wooden horses on merry-go-rounds, they merely go around in circles.

In their personal lives they tend to lead uneventful existences. At work, if discussions come up involving issues of cultural diversity, they often change the subject or discount its importance or act as if they are bored with the challenges and problems that cultural diversity brings to an organization.

Bosses with banal scripts expect "the show" to be mediocre. Being hopelessly uninspired, they don't believe they could develop sufficient skill and creativity — in themselves or in others — to put on a first-rate performance. Bosses with banal scripts often work for organizations that are also banal. They are slow to adapt to a changing multicultural workforce and slow to introduce innovative procedures, products or services.

Constructive scripts are the scripts of winners. Bosses and organizations with constructive scripts are concerned about their employees whether they are on or off the job. They value multiculturalism and would like to see more of it at top management levels.

These kinds of bosses can be recognized by their effectiveness because they act from the plus side of their bossing skills. They share the stage and the spotlight with others, write positive letters about employees for their files and actively seek to promote those who are qualified — regardless of race, ethnicity or gender.

They work against situations that contribute to poverty, disease, discrimination and other tragedies that lead to unhealthiness and unhappiness. They are committed to leaving the world-stage a better one for having had a part in the drama.

Granted, many organizations, especially businesses, are primarily concerned with making money. Yet as James Liebig points out, some also have altruistic goals, have an honest concern for the development and well-being of individuals and of society as a whole.

Their constructive scripts are expressed through ethical management, social responsibility, and the involvement of employees at every level. Employee involvement may take the form of stock ownership in the company so their effectiveness can enrich them directly.

Involvement may also be encouraged in regular meetings with management so employees can express their dissatisfactions without fear of reprisal and where their ideas for improving the organization are taken seriously. Today, every good or better boss knows that decisions made only from the top of a hierarchical structure stand the risk of failing.

Psychological positions and script themes

In addition to its basic constructiveness or lack of it, a script has a theme that shows up again and again in the four psychological positions that a person takes. Week after week these themes can be spotted.

Confident (I'm OK, you're OK) bosses tend to get along with people by being trustworthy and authentic. They often have script themes such as "from one success to another," "acquiring friends not enemies," and "being responsible and fun."

Egotistical (I'm OK but you are not-OK) bosses tend to get rid of people by putting them off or putting them down. Themes of egotistical bosses include "acting like a big shot," "treating subordinates as if they were not important," and "trying to get rid of a culturally diverse staff."

Insecure (I'm not-OK but you are OK) bosses tend to get away from people. Script themes of insecure bosses include: "never doing anything quite right," "putting too much energy into unimportant things," "being mediocre," and "getting criticized."

Hopeless (I'm not-OK and you're not-OK either) bosses tend to give up on people by not expecting anything positive from them or from themselves. Script themes of hopeless bosses include "not getting anything done," "making major mistakes," "driving people crazy," and "giving up."

The origin of personal scripts

Scripts are selected so early in life that they are in place before a child is even aware of choosing a role. If a child is wanted, if the parents are physically and emotionally healthy, if the birth is normal, if the parents are pleased with the sex and appearance of the child, then the child is likely to begin life feeling good. Such a child is likely to select a positive I'm OK, you're OK script, cope constructively with the difficulties of growing up, and later in life become an effective and well-liked boss.

On the other hand, if a child is not wanted, if something goes wrong during pregnancy or birth, if the parents feel resentful, frustrated or angry at the responsibility, or disappointed in the sex or appearance of the child, the child is likely to begin life feeling not-OK and may select a destructive script that matches the feeling.

Many children get mixed messages and conclude they're partly OK and partly not-OK. Those that get these mixed messages tend to fluctuate in their job performance and in their feelings of self-esteem. They often feel that whatever they do is not quite good enough. The net effect is they live by banal scripts.

Work and gender scripting

Many early experiences lead to script decisions about work. Girls who get the message that "Women's place is in the home" may feel guilty when they leave the home to work. Boys who get the same message about women may believe that women who work outside the home would be better off if they stayed home.

Another common script about working is the parental message that "Men are supposed to be the boss." Some men are effective bosses, but not all. In today's multicultural world, the better organizations are promoting women, too, into top management positions. Its a big problem when women are serving in the fighting forces, a woman is chief of police at the University of California, yet women not accepted as equals at the Naval Academy.

This issue of work and gender is often a problem for men who have been taught in childhood to assume sexual dominance of women in their personal lives and get gender preference for the better managerial jobs at work. Such a man may try very hard to keep women under his control. Thus, the early childhood script is played out.

"Be a man!" is a common script command of parents who want a son to act tough and hide his soft feelings. As anthropologist David Gilmore notes, in most societies men are supposed to impregnate women, protect dependents and provide for the family. Manhood is often thought of as something that has to be won in some kind of ritual involving pain. Different cultures have different criteria for what the ideal man should be but the most common one is the belief that he should be tough, brave, virile and stoic, even when in great pain.

These beliefs are no longer as nearly universal as they once were. When the gentle Tahitians and timid Senoi men are considered, than it seems clear that aggressiveness and dominance are, at least partly scripted, not entirely inborn as often taught.

The down-scripting of women

Women are the largest subcultural group that exists, larger than those defined by race, ethnicity or age. Yet they have often considered themselves to be unimportant in the work place and have accepted the down-scripted role of Victim.

Historically, in the United States women have had many duties but few rights. They have been culturally scripted to be supporting characters, stage hands or applauding audiences for male achievements and men's dramas. They have been encouraged to avoid the spotlight, to avoid "promoting" themselves, to avoid using authority at home unless delegated to them, and to avoid jobs commonly thought of as masculine.

In the United States change began slowly in 1838 when women were first allowed to vote in school elections in Kentucky. It was not until 1964, in the House of Representatives, that an amendment was passed that added women's rights to the Civil Rights Bill. The original Bill prohibited discrimination on the basis of "race, color, religion or national origin." The amendment proposed that the word "sex" be added to the anti-discrimination clause. Ridicule and shouts of laughter met this proposal, but it passed by a small margin. One hundred thirty-three representatives were against it and one hundred and sixty-eight were in favor of women having equal rights.

Yet women have not won equal opportunities. Like many in the so-called minority groups, they have had to fight for equality. Things may be changing. Today many women and organizations are by choice or by law rewriting these kinds of "stay-down" scripts. They no longer enjoy the same old acts with the sexist roles that were so banal.

The theater at work

Although the roles of some people are less obvious than others, all people act at times as though they were reading lines that should go in a theatrical script and were written by someone else.

In every script there are many factors similar to those in stage dramas. There are producers, main characters and supporting characters and the dialogue that goes on among them. There are scenes and acts with special lighting and scenery to fit the drama.

Parents are the original producers in each person's life, (though there are others.) The others are usually the "big" bosses who may be on stage directing the show, or off-stage managing the directors or coaches. Although the big bosses may delegate authority to others for hiring the characters, setting the scene, funding the production and advising on promotion, they often keep the power of making the final decisions for themselves.

Many scripts call for the same kind of characters that are found in games. The difference between a game role and a script role is that in games a person switches from one role to another. In scripts they tend to stay in one. Thus, the games people play are like short scenes that advance a life drama.

Subordinates on any job are often perceived as supporting characters to their bosses. As such, they are likely to have peripheral positions on stage. They are also expected to substitute or "back-up" those in the field or in the head office.

Regardless of where employees are in the line of command, they have their individual and collective dramas.

Between the time when the curtain rises and the curtain falls the characters act and speak in various ways according to the preprogrammed script. Even the language and accents are scripted and this sometimes creates a farce, a tragedy or a comedy. Many companies have lost their international markets because the words in their advertising slogans were disastrously translated into other languages.

Because language is a part of every script, the necessity of studying foreign languages in rapidly increasing in multicultural organizations. This is particularly important in those organizations that are involved in international business and political affairs.

It is common to hear politicians from other countries on TV speaking English with great fluency. The reverse is not true. There is a story about President Reagan who, after making a speech, enthusiastically applauded the next speaker until he was told that the speaker was just translating what Reagan had said. Embarrassing moments are experienced by about everyone who venture across international borders, especially if the language is not understood.

Even the style of dressing, whether the style is to wear a suit, a sari or jeans, can reflect ethnic scripts and the scripts of an organization. "Dressing for the part" is often part of a job that characters act out. It may contribute to the whole play. The news anchors or political figures on TV often spend considerable time on their clothes and make-up because they want to present a particular image to the public. Their gestures and facial expressions are often carefully planned to appeal to the largest audience. They have only a certain time on stage and want to make the most of it.

The scenario of every drama includes the games people play. During games the players act out their chosen roles. The drama moves on to a climax, a denouement and final curtain. The audience applauds, boos, or yawns.

Even a detail such as lighting may be a significant part of the script. There are two basic kinds of lighting for stage dramas: spotlights that focus on a central character or scene, and floodlights that light up the whole stage. Dishonest bosses or employees will tend to avoid either kind of light so that they can work without being observed by others. Hostile or creative bosses or employees may "upstage" others to get the lion's share of the spotlight, and bosses with the "team spirit" will want the whole company to be in floodlights.

Scenery is also important, and organizations that want to announce some kind of change often do so by changing the scenery. Scenery varies from bleakness to vividness. One suburban bank changed its scenery by painting its walls in three shades of bright orange. Complaints, errors, absenteeism and personnel turnover increased. After two months the walls were repainted with softer colors and business began to pick up again.

An automobile agency in the same town changed its dull image by adding colorful carpeting, amusing murals, and wide open spaces between desks. Employees were given some freedom to decorate their own scenes. Potential buyers enjoyed going there, as the scenery contributed to a good show.

But when people speak of wanting a "change of scenery," they seldom mean simply a wall or rug color. They more often mean they would prefer a different stage setting, different characters, and a different drama than the one being staged. Thus they may go on vacation, get a divorce, or change jobs depending upon the direction and intensity of their dislike for things being the way they have been.

Cultural scripts

All cultures have scripts. The cultural script is the expected
and accepted dramatic patterns that occur within a society.
These patterns are determined by the spoken and unspoken
assumptions of the majority of the people within that group or
assumptions that are imposed on the group by powerful
figures.

A long and eventful cultural script is that of the Native
Americans who migrated to North America across the Bering
Straights over 30,000 years ago. Originally their script theme
was living-off-the-land by hunting and gathering. Then as the
weather got warmer with the ending of the ice age, they developed a taking-care- of-the-land agricultural script by planting
corn and cotton. By 1,000 A.D. the Pueblo tribe had changed
its script again, from agriculture to urban development,
building-upon-the-land with apartments of stone that had as
many as nine hundred rooms.

Originally their script was self-determined. Then a new one was
imposed by the Spaniards who wanted to make them
Christians and slaves, and by the French who wanted to trade
with them. In 1763, the English designated all the land west of
the Appalachians as belonging to the Native Americans. But
taking away of that land began in 1830 with a series of acts that
nullified their claims, resulted in bloody wars, and sent most of
the Native Americans to live on reservations. A new script was
imposed on them, "Live where ever you're sent with whatever
you're given to live with."

Currently, strong Native American voices are emerging who
are working to "rescript" their people to self- determination
and wholeness instead of fragmentation and despair. And it
won't be easy. Large government organizations always have
their own scripts and the organizations are generally run by
parent type bosses who, if concerned about maintaining power,
often deny wrong-doing and resist change.

In addition to the cultural scripts of a nation or race, there are subcultural scripts that are defined by geography, language, religion, sex, race, ethnicity, or some other way. The family unit is the smallest subculture. Through the family the scripts of the national culture are often passed down, generation after generation. For example, when the United States was being formed, it developed a "work hard" script, often called the "Protestant work ethic" because of the hard work that was necessary for the mostly Protestant immigrants who were seeking a better life.

Although hard work has become less popular as the culture has become more affluent, it is still a strong script theme in many business corporations. In government and non-profit organizations where tenure is the rule, the script of working hard may be somewhat less common for those of European descent but many Asians have work-hard scripts and this too impacts the larger culture.

Assimilation and pluralism

One of the questions facing many immigrants and refugees is whether to maintain their cultural and sub- cultural values or find ways to be assimilated in the larger culture. This question comes up at work as well as in social situations.

Assimilation is the blending of groups. People from different backgrounds try to blend in and become more like people of the larger culture. They may change their names, customs, style of dress, even hairstyles so that they fit into the established culture.

Pluralism is just the opposite; it implies cultural variety rather than similarity. Although people from various cultures may be in contact with one another, they maintain their separate identities — their own scripts. This separatism is often expressed by people who keep their names, their customs and traditions, and elements of their native dress. They do not want to change these things because they want to keep their cultural identity rather than be assimilated.

In many work situations there are some employees who prefer pluralism and some who prefer assimilation. At one time it was more common to seek assimilation at work and maintain cultural tradition at home. Now, as times change, many do not want to hide their personal preferences or adopt another culture. They are pleased with their own uniqueness.

In Canada, for example, many of those who live in Quebec prefer to be called French Canadians to indicate their cultural roots; and some want political as well as cultural independence for Quebec. A similar movement in Eastern Europe reflects scripts of other people who want political self-determination as the only way to maintain the integrity of their culture.

The term "Native Americans" is now commonly used for people who were once called Indians. Mexican Americans are claiming their national subcultural heritage in the wider category of Hispanics. Currently, many people who were once called Negroes, then Blacks, are choosing to be called African Americans. Perhaps, as more pride is taken in cultural backgrounds, other groups will define themselves as Irish Americans or German Americans or European Americans.

Whereas these designations may please those who want them, they may not work in the world-wide culture of today because people from Central America, South America, and Canada find it pretty irritating when USA citizens use "American" to describe themselves as if the rest of America did not exist.

As for those whose ancestors were among the first to migrate, they may say something like, "My ancestors came over on the Mayflower" or "My ancestors fought in the revolutionary war."

Because they have been rooted in the United States for so long, this may lead to a egotistical position towards others or it may lead to a more open and welcoming attitude toward others.

The United States has often been called a "melting pot." The phrase came from a play by Israel Zanwill of England who, in

1908, used the image for the United States as a crucible where Europeans would become a new race. The analogy has become debatable as each wave of immigrants brings its own cultural background and sometimes chooses to maintain its distinctive qualities. A few years ago a small urban bank in a predominately Jewish neighborhood was bought by an English firm and a new organizational script line was whispered around among employees. It was, "Talk British but think Yiddish."

Not only names, customs and life styles reflect cultural diversity. Religion provides other kinds of scripts that often are important to many. Christmas and Easter were first established as legal holidays so that the largest religious group could have time to worship. Today, on the basis of separation of church and state, those who are not Christian sometimes protest at public funds being used to recognize these celebrations. Those who do not have any religious affiliation may feel the same, or be indifferent to the religious purpose but glad of the holiday.

Tensions between religious organizations do not always affect politics. As religious cultures change, so do political ones. When John F. Kennedy ran for the office of the president of the United States, many claimed it was impossible for him to become president because he was Catholic in a country founded by Protestants. Obviously, they were wrong.

Effective and efficient scripting

The ways people act are often determined by the culture which, functioning like a director of the drama, says, "This is the way it's supposed to be." Consequently, many people of a specific race, ethnic background, age, sex and so forth, are scripted by their culture to do certain kinds of jobs with a certain level of authority. Better bosses and organizations break up this kind of typecasting, promoting on the basis of individual effectiveness, not on the basis of a stereotype.

To keep the good show going, effective bosses may rewrite the script, fire some of the "stars" or supporting characters and hire new ones. They may develop new dialogue to replace banal cliches and update going-nowhere scenes and acts. They are authentic and choose to be themselves instead of playing roles.

Effective bosses who are better than the average also know their personal scripts and use the constructive parts of them. They know the script of their organization and how it affects their employees. When they are on the job, they direct, coach, delegate, analyze, negotiate, advocate and innovate in ways that contribute to a good show in which employees want to participate. They are well-liked personally and professionally and applauded in one way or another for their positive bossing styles. They are leaders.

Self-discovery

To get in touch with your personal script try asking yourself the questions:

- What happens to people who like me who...?

- What will happen next if I go on as I now am? (A clue to the next scene or act).

- What will be the logical conclusions of my acting this way? (A clue to the possible final curtain of your life drama).

When psychological scripts are being played out, characters interact with each other according to what the director tells them to do. How about you?

- Is your personal script generally constructive, destructive or banal?

- What roles do you play most often and where?

- Who seems to be directing your show?

What about your cultural script?

- What are some of the slogans or life styles that you have given up or maintained for yourself?

- Do your racial, national or gender scripts have a history of competitiveness with others or submission to them?

- If so, does this old script affect your job in any way?

For discovering the scripts of business corporations, government agencies and non-profit organizations, ask:

- What happens to organizations that function as we do?

- Is our organization on a destructive trend, on a going-nowhere road or does it have success in sight?

How does your personal script interact with the scripts of your culture and the organization for whom you work? Are you satisfied?

So what to do

The things that happen to bosses and employees over and over again are brief scenes in their scripts. These things are usually related in some way to what happened in their childhood and are like replays of earlier scenes.

Some people, instead of living by the scripts they picked out for themselves, live out their parents' scripts. These are people who constantly function from a Parent ego state or from an Adult ego state which is contaminated by Parent traditions or Child feelings and adaptations. Other people stay stuck in the Child ego state and with the script decisions they made years ago.

To rewrite your script, imagine yourself as a young child on a stage. See again the characters that were on stage with you, the dialogue and action, the kind of show it was. Were you in the spotlight or not? If so, in what way? If not, why not? What do you conclude?

Now, see yourself on one or more of the stages on which you act in your current life. Who's there? What's the drama going on? Is it constructive, destructive or merely banal?

Is there anything you'd like to do differently?

Rewriting a script often requires redeciding that which was decided in childhood. Whereas childhood decisions may have survival value at the time they are made, they frequently do not apply in later life. Nor do all cultural and parental traditions.

The better bosses change negative decisions that are "ancient history." They let go of the past in favor of new positive decisions that are made for the here and now and for a successful future. They are also confident that organizational scripts which are out of date can also be changed and do what they can to change them.

8

Time for contracts

Fair but not equal

There is a difference between a manager who does a pretty good job of managing and one who manages well because of being a leader. The old cliche, "Leaders are born, not made" is untrue. All people have leadership potential. Whether or not they become leaders can depend on their willingness to look objectively at their strengths and weaknesses and take personal responsibility for improving themselves.

Organizations have hierarchies, yet those at the top are not necessarily leaders. Employees may resist following them and may do so only because it is necessary. The kinds of bosses that employees are more likely to follow are those that encourage others and treat them fairly but not equally.

Speaking rapidly to all employees may be treating them equally but to those who are still learning to speak a new language, it is not giving them a "fair chance to understand." communication. Even when people know a language well, they often use words in different ways. When Japanese say "yes," it does not always mean agreement. Sometimes it means "I hear you."

For effective communication it seldom makes sense to treat all employees equally. The formality or informality of a boss's interpersonal relations on the job can be offensive or pleasing, depending upon the cultural values of those involved. One employee may appreciate a friendly clap on the shoulder, another can be deeply offended by it. One may thrive in an informal atmosphere where there is much freedom to make independent decisions, another feel very uncomfortable at the lack of firm structure. The better bosses are those who are alert to differences in cultures and alert to the need to respect them.

This alertness comes from the awareness that different people respond more positively to one kind of boss than to another. As Copeland and Griggs point out, French, Italian, and German executives are expected to make the decisions, because "that's what they're paid to do." With the British, the same expectation is rooted in class consciousness, while with Japanese employees participatory group decision-making is expected. And Arabs do not like group process in decision-making but prefer person-to-person consultation.

Of course these generalities are not always applicable. but the better boss will be aware of them as possibilities that require the ability to change bossing styles easily.

Culture and time

Bosses often consider time to be one of their most precious commodities and it is common for organizations to use time clocks that record the minute a worker shows up and leaves a job. This custom is very difficult for some people of other cultures to understand. The Swiss are as punctual as their famous trains. But to people from Mexico or other Latin countries the idea of being punctual is quite alien.

Manuel Palo explained it to a co-worker, "It is almost impossible to plan to be anywhere at a certain time in Mexico City; the traffic is too bad. So we just say something like I'll be there more or less around nine or ten o'clock. That means we would show up anytime between eight or eleven."

Even the words for time are used differently in some languages than in English or German. In Spanish and Arabian, words that translate tomorrow really mean soon.

In workshops for military or ex-military personnel a coffee break of ten minutes is interpreted to mean ten minutes, not nine or eleven. Setting such a tight schedule for most other groups simply would not work and trainers who do so would likely be seen by others as demanding directors when they perceive themselves as encouraging coaches.

For many people, using time to work is not as important as using time to socialize. They see the purpose of work is to support society so they work enough to live, but do not live to work. Bosses who negotiate international issues often learn that long social conversations or ritual exchanges before negotiates start are often necessary for success. On a less formal basis, "social" interactions may be very important to employee stress reduction and good functioning.

Brian Slatter was an enforcer of rules and strongly believed in "running a tight ship." When he became manager in a district office of a public utility company, he insisted on changes. He staggered check-in times and lunch breaks so that friends who worked in the same office building had great difficulty making connections. When he wanted to regiment even the coffee breaks, Yuri Kataya, his top computer programmer abruptly resigned. Enough was enough.

The rush to use time to "get something done" can seriously interfere with reflective time for considering values and creative innovations. Providing time for training is not considered important by some bosses who claim, "It takes away time from the job." Other bosses, more aware of the need for training, sometimes hope that a one-day training course can effectively change the misconceptions and prejudices that have existed for many years. It may help, but an on-going program is likely to be more effective.

Time and its uses are big issues for corporations and there are six basic ways people structure their time when they are with others. They use rituals, pastimes and games; they work together in various kinds of activities, enjoy each other in authentic relationships and sometimes withdraw into daydreaming and fantasy.

Managers, using the positive side of any bossing skill are likely to respect the rituals of meeting and greeting and the recognition of employees with positive strokes. In some situations, a "hello" from a boss carries a lot of weight.

Overly busy bosses, playing games such as *Overworked Executive*, sometimes act as though rituals were a "waste of time." Rituals, as minimal forms of recognition, are necessary in any kind of situation.

Pastimes are extended conversations at a somewhat casual level about subjects such as sports, weather, cars, kids, vacations, and so forth. They often are extensions of rituals. For example, during the ritual of a coffee break, pastiming is common. In fact, it is so deeply ingrained in many work situations that not having it would be interpreted by some as the breaking of a "sacred" tradition. The criticism against pastimes was that they can "eat up so much time" and interfere with "getting the job done."

Psychological games are usually the most unproductive use of time because of their ulterior purposes. When games are over, someone is likely to have collected negative feelings. Games interfere with problem-solving and decision-making. They diminish feelings of loyalty and the sense of trust.

When bosses or subordinates are indifferent or bored with what's going on, they often withdraw into fantasies, everything from shopping binges to fishing trips to what they would do if they were the "big bosses." If they sense that they are expected to look busy when the boss comes by, they may suddenly shuffle a flurry of papers, while pretending to be involved when actually they couldn't care less about a dull or difficult report.

Open, honest relationships with a minimum of ulterior transactions often lead to a sense of closeness and appreciation among those working as a team.

Although such intimacy feels good for those who are involved, it can be negative to those who observe it in others but do not feel included. This continues to be a problem in multicultural situations, because being left out is so easily attributed to prejudice and cultural differences when sometimes it is not.

Better managers may not like everyone equally but they know that fairness is essential in team building. They recognize that being friendly with one person may be perceived as "playing favorites" by others and that this can have a demoralizing effect on those who feel themselves to be less popular.

Therefore, whenever possible, good bosses express appreciation to all employees. Their minimal game-playing increases motivation and harmony.

With the need to be sensitive to so many issues, a boss can feel overwhelmed. To cope with this feeling, the ability to make contracts is one of the most useful tools for improving bossing skills.

Theory of contracts

Contracts are strategic agreements to do something about something. They contain details of what, when, where, how, and with whom. They can be made with oneself or with others. Contracts take time to establish because the terms often need to be thought through carefully to be effective.

Contracts are plans of action to which a person is committed. On the job a boss can make self-contracts such as to complete a delayed report, or to confront an employee who is continually late, or to take time out for a vacation, or review a budget, or to learn more about how language and customs in multicultural workplaces impact the job.

This can be very crucial in joint ventures such as the new one between Chrysler Corporation and Mitsubishi Motor Corporation. Think of how many misunderstandings are possible because so many plurals are used in the English language, but in Japanese the only plural words used are "children" and "friends."

In personal life as well as at work, misunderstandings occur and contracts are also useful. They can be established to change any behavior, for example, to stop procrastinating on a chore at home and start completing projects as scheduled.

Contracts can be established to change feelings; for example, to stop feeling like a Victim when criticized and to start listening and evaluating criticism realistically. Or to stop feeling the need to Rescue or Persecute others and instead find ways to get others to take more responsibility for themselves.

Contracts can also be made to improve one's health, to decrease psychosomatic symptoms such as overweight or high blood pressure, and to start respecting one's own body and feelings. Unless contracts for self-care are made and kept, the life of any individual can be at risk.

The contracts made for one's personal life inevitably affect the job; those made for work can greatly impact one's social life.

Many people do not make valid contracts because they are tied to destructive or banal scripts, or they lack information or sensitivity.

Tim O'Malley was six feet-five inches tall and the manager of a large office. When he was assigned several new employees from Hong Kong, he had difficulty conveying his ideas to them. One day in desperation he sat down alongside one of their desks. Immediately communication improved, and he realized that some of the interpersonal discomfort was due, not to racial differences, but to his height, which to others was sometimes intimidating. He made a contract with himself to stay aware of this kind of potential problem.

Requirements of contracts

The purpose of learning how to make contracts is to deliberately change what can be changed to improve life and work. When people make contracts, they use a particular process designed to facilitate change.

For contracts to be effective they need to be clear, precise and direct. They also need to be based on realistic goals which can be reached by realistic means.

For instance, a realistic contract can be made about learning to speak a foreign language, but it is not realistic to expect to be proficient in a month or two. A realistic contract can be made about getting a better job but it may not be realistic to expect to get it without experience.

One can make a realistic contract to look more attractive, but at fifty it is not realistic to try to pass for twenty. But an organization that is youth oriented, looking older than one must may be part of a banal, going nowhere script.

One of the current myths is that it is necessary for bosses who become leaders to be charismatic as well as very attractive. Research show this is not true. Charisma may lead to good sales but, in the long run, authenticity is more important; the willingness to be honest and respectful of self and others is more persuasive than a fine facade.

To complete a contract successfully, some kind of external or internal change is necessary. Therefore the willingness to change is a major requirement. Many bosses say they are in favor of change but all too often that means they want other people to change rather than changing themselves.

Dolores Ruiz did not have this problem. Her family background did not encourage success but she decided to succeed anyway. At age twenty-three Dolores began as a bank teller and set realistic goals for herself. She attended night school two nights a week to study business and economics. Gradually she was given more responsibility, became a branch manager and when she was forty-one years old was made one of the four women vice presidents of the state-wide banking firm.

In every contract some kind of personal change is necessary. To improve communication on the job for example, many bosses need to stop blaming others for "not understanding." They need to take responsibility for their part of daily transactions and make them fit the persons involved and the situations. They need to ask themselves, "What can I do differently that will be effective, efficient, and ethical?"

Making personal contracts

The heart of successful contracting is the use of five questions and careful evaluation of the answers.

First comes the establishment of a goal with the question, "What do I want that would enhance my life or work?" This question is designed to admit that bosses have personal as well as professional goals and that bringing these goals into clear awareness is the first step to change.

Second comes the question, "What would I need to change so that I could get what I want?" This question recognizes that personal change, not just changing others, is necessary. Of course, others may change in the process but that's not the focus of this question.

Third is, "What would I be willing to do to make the change happen?" This is recognizing that change in a situation usually starts with one person who is willing to do something about it, instead of just sitting around complaining and blaming. If someone is not willing to take responsibility, the contract will not be kept. It will be like a New Year Eve's resolution, soon forgotten.

The next step is to ask, "How will I know when I am successful and how will it show to others?" This is recognizing the fact that personal evaluation and feedback from others are essential to reinforce positive changes.

The fifth step is to question, "How might I sabotage or undermine myself so that I would not achieve my goals?" This is recognizing how inner dialogue, or transactions with others, or games that are played, or scripts that are acted out, might interfere with the successful completion of a contract.

A boss and employee contract

A similar process is required in order to effect change between two people or to encourage an employee to change something that may need changing. In this situation, the boss often uses statements, followed by questions which are followed by discussion. A contract setting session might go as follows:

"Stan, the company has set a goal for us to increase production 12 percent . Would you be willing to agree with this goal?" If Stan answers "yes," the contract-making can continue. If not, then a discussion might reveal some problems that could interfere with reaching the company goal.

Next comes, "Stan, is there anything that needs changing so that this goal could be reached?" Discussion would then follow.

Third comes, "I'm wondering if there's something you could do, Stan, and would be willing to do to make this change happen?" More discussion.

Then, "What kind of evaluation or feedback do you think is needed so that others in the organization would be aware of the change?" Again, more talk.

Next, "How might the goal and the process be sabotaged?" or "Who might do what, that would interfere with success?"

When making contracts with other people, it is essential that each point be discussed in order and that time be available for discussion.

Bosses who play *Harried* and claim they "don't have enough time to think things over again" or enough time to "talk it through," are sabotaging themselves, their employees and their organization.

A caution on contracts

Sometimes bosses and employees, in a flurry of enthusiasm, make unrealistic contracts. Like people who make New Year's Eve resolutions, they do not evaluate their commitment to change. Consequently, their good intentions are short-lived.

Writing down the answers to each of the five contract steps is one way to avoid this kind of failure. It is important, however, to continually review and evaluate as the contract progresses. Sometimes the Parent and Child ego states interfere with this Adult process.

A person's Parent ego state might undermine the process by sending messages such as "Keep on working," (in other words, "Don't stop to think about what you're working on.") The Child might undermine the process by responding "See how hard I'm working," (in other words, "See how obedient I am by not questioning the value of what I do.")

Unless the boss is alert, these messages from the Parent and Child can contaminate the Adult decision to make and keep a contract. Writing down the contracts that one makes with one-self or others, and then periodically reviewing them, is an effective way to sabotage any potential saboteur - whether it is another boss or a subordinate.

Effective and efficient contracts

Successful bosses who are in constructive scripts use time in many ways. When they make their "to do" list, they give priority to important issues and the people they care about.

For instance, Lila Mae Davis established a reasonable contract: Instead of being an anxious appeaser type she decided to become a dynamic speaker so that she could present her ideas more forcefully to upper management. To achieve this goal, she had to change her habit of mumbling. She made that change by staying aware of when she was doing it and taking a public-speaking course. She is also practiced with a tape recorder in front of a mirror. Others knew that she had changed when she successfully negotiated a schedule change for the group she was supervising. Lila Mae could have undermined her self-contract by being "too busy," or "too scared," or "too tired" to attend the public speaking course. She did not allow herself to do that as she had decided to be a better boss. Her contract was successful because it was specific and has a definite plan of action. It was reasonable and practical.

Managers like Lila Mae manage time well and are willing to make contracts with others which will enhance the quality of life. They seldom play games and avoid lengthy "pastiming" and going-nowhere rituals which are characteristic of people who have banal scripts. Yet they also realize that the value placed on these kinds of activities differ from culture to culture.

They know their own priorities and set contracts to achieve them. They care about people including themselves, and show their caring in appropriate ways. They communicate with confidence by using their positive bossing skills.

Self-discovery

One of the most common complaints of bosses at all organizational levels is that they don't have enough time. If you feel like that, consider the following:

- Out of the one hundred and sixty-eight hours available to you each week, how many do you spend in sleeping?

- Preparing meals and eating them?

- Shopping and personal grooming?

- Family responsibilities? Chores around home?

- Watching TV? Other forms of pleasure or relaxation?

- Actually working on the job? Commuting to work?

On the basis of the above, do you need a contract about how you spend your time?

- What do you want that would enhance your life and job?

- What would you need to do to get it?

- What are you willing to do to get what you want?

- What would you need to change?

Now, to review how each of your ego states is involved in how you structure your time, consider:

- What are the opinions from your Parent ego state opinion about your use of time?

- How would your Adult ego state analyze your use of time?

- How does your Child feel about your use of time?

By any chance, do you need a contract to restructure your time and take more time out for you to increase your basic OKness on the job?

So what to do

It's not easy to contract to change oneself, and it's not easy to get someone else involved in changing, but both can be done. An effective way to get into contracting is to start with small goals and achieve them before moving on to something larger.

With contracting, you can take more control of your life. You can contract to listen with your Adult to your own inner dialogue. You may hear an inner voice saying something like, "You'll never do anything right!" This comes from your inner Parent ego state beating up on your Child. Or, you may hear something like, "I can't do it and I wouldn't even dare try." This would be your apologetic, fearful Child. With awareness you can use your Adult effectively to referee in this kind of inner dialogue.

You can also contract to transact more openly, using complementary transactions when possible, and crossing game transactions when they become harmful.

You can contract to use your time for you. You don't always have to say "yes" when you want to say "no." You can choose who to spend time with in activities and intimacy and who to avoid.

The better boss

The better boss is one who makes choices. You can decide what kind of bossing style you want to use now. Next year. Five years from now. Also, what kind of a job you want now. Next year. Five years from now.

Look at what needs changing. Decide what you're willing to do, set up a time schedule, and do it. Enjoy the job:

> Direct, as a discerning boss
>
> Coach, as an encouraging boss

Delegate, as an empowering boss

Analyze, as a caring boss

Make peace, as a negotiating boss

Defend, as an advocating boss

Innovate, as a creative boss

All effective and efficient bosses are flexible. They figure out the best ways to maximize their own potential and the potentials of others. They recognize the great value of cultural diversity.

Regardless of the bossing skills they use most often, they use them from the positive side with the confident belief, "I'm OK, you're OK." They are winners and believe that others were also born to win. They believe that any form of discrimination can be given up in favor of ethics, authenticity and appreciation.

For further reading

Allport, Gordon. *The Nature of Prejudice*. Reading, Massachusetts: Addison-Wesley Publishing. Originally published 1954. Republished 1988.

Bell, Derrick. *And We Are Not Saved: The Elusive Quest ForRacial Justice*. New York: Basic Books, 1987.

Brown, D. *Bury My Heart at Wounded Knee: An Indian History of the American West*. New York: Holt, Rinehart & Winston, 1970.

Copeland, Lennie & Lewis Griggs. *Going International: How to Make Friends and Deal Effectively in the Global Marketplace*. New York: Plume Books, NAL, 1986.

Drucker, Peter. *Managing the Non-Profit Organization: Practices and Principles*. New York: Harper Collins, 1990.

Fischer, David Hackett. *Albion's Seed*. Oxford University Press, 1989.

Eliot, Robert S. & Dennis Breo. *Is it Worth Dying For?* New York: Bantam, 1984.

Garcia, Mario T. *Mexican Americans: Leadership. Ideology, & Identity: 1930 - 1960*. Yale University Press, 1989.

Gardner, John W. *Leadership*. New York: Macmillan, Free Press, 1990.

Gilmore, David D. *Manhood in the Making: Cultural Concepts of Manhood*.

Grier, William & Price Cobbs. *Black Rage*. New York: Basic Books, 1968.

James, Muriel & Dorothy Jongeward, *Born to Win: Transactional Analysis With Gestalt Experiments*. Reading, Massachusetts: Addison-Wesley Publishing, 1971.

Liebig, James. *Business Ethics: Profiles in Civic Virtue.* Golden, Colorado: Fulcrum Publishing, 1990.

Nakano, Mei, *Japanese American Women: Three Generations; 1800-1990.* Sabastopol, California: Mina Press Publishing and Nat'l Japanese American Historical Society, San Francisco, 1990.

Ohmae, Kenichi, *The Mind of the Strategist.* New York: Penguin Books, 1982.

Petersen, William, Michael Novak, & Philip Gleason. *Concepts of Ethnicity.* Cambridge, Massachusetts: Belknap Press of Harvard University Press, 1982.

Takaki, Ronald. *Strangers From a Different Shore: A History of Asian Americans.* New York: Little, Brown & Co., 1989.

Toffler, Alvin. *Powershift.* New York: Bantam, 1990.

Portes, Alejandro and Robert L. Bach. *Latin Journey: Cuban and Mexican Immigrants in the United States.* Berkeley, California: University of California Press, 1985.

About the author

Muriel James grew up in San Francisco and has her doctorate from the University of California in Berkeley in the psychology of adult learning with her doctoral thesis in intercultural crises in ancient history. She continues to enjoy studying in diverse-fields.

Dr. James is author or coauthor of 17 books, translated into many languages, including the four million bestseller *Born To Win: Transactional Analysis with Gestalt Experiences* which is translated into sixteen languages. In addition to *The Better Boss,* her other new books are *Hearts on Fire: Romances in the Lives of Great Women* and *Passion for Life: Psychology and Human Spirit.* In addition to books, she has written numerous articles and has been featured in audio and video programs.

A lecturer and consultant in human relations for businesses, government agencies, and mental health organizations around the world. Muriel is a pioneer in the field of Transactional Analysis and Gestalt Therapy, past president of the International Transactional Analysis Association, member of the American Group Psychotherapy Association and the International Group Psychotherapy Association.

She has led workshops for organizations as diverse as NASA, U. S. Navy, American Medical Association, University of Vienna, CITA Switzerland, Bank of America, University of Buenos Aires, AT&T, Wells Fargo Bank, Xerox, IBM, World Council of Churches, Swiss Air, Tata Motors India, Lufthansa Airlines, University of Pacific School of Dentistry, National Association of Social Workers, Institute for the Advancement of Human Behavior, American Association of Therapeutic Humor, Young President's Organization,and many more. She also served as a mediator in cross-cultural high school crises and was an advisor to the first California Commission on the Status of Women.

Previous to her career as an author, psychotherapist and educator she had a multitude of jobs. Her first, at age sixteen, was singing with a big band at the Fairmont Hotel in San Francisco; later she modeled wedding gowns. She was also on the staff of the Red Cross, a shipyard safety engineer, public school teacher, university faculty member.

She has been on many national television shows,including "Good Morning America," "A.M. New York," "Today Show," and CNN's "Nightwatch," and has been interviewed on TV by people such as Hugh Downs, Sonia Friedman, Regis Philbin, and Jack Webster, and for many radio programs, magazines and newspapers. Her lecturing and leading workshops has taken her to over forty countries.

Muriel is married and the mother of three grown children and stepmother to four more.